Jonathan M. Kli[c]

University of Maryland at College Park

STUDY GUIDE AND MAP WORKBOOK

Out of Many

THIRD EDITION

A History of the American People
Volume Two

John Mack Faragher
Yale University

Mari Jo Buhle
Brown University

Daniel Czitrom
Mount Holyoke College

Susan H. Armitage
Washington State University

PRENTICE HALL, *Upper Saddle River, NJ 07458*

© 2000 by PRENTICE-HALL, INC.
Upper Saddle River, New Jersey 07458

10987654321

ISBN 0-13-999574-9
Printed in the United States of America

TABLE OF CONTENTS

PREFACE TO THE STUDENT: STUDY FORMAT

This study guide is meant to complement, not replace, the textbook *Out of Many: A History of the American People*, 3rd edition by John Mack Faragher, Mari Jo Buhle, Daniel Czitrom, and Susan H. Armitage. If used effectively, your study of American history should proceed more efficiently and effectively.

Before you begin reading each chapter, it would be profitable to review both the relevant **Chapter Overview** and **Chapter Objectives** sections contained in this study guide. These sections will serve as your map to the text which, due to the wealth of information it contains, can often become overwhelming. By knowing where it is you are headed before hand, your journey through the text will be greatly simplified.

While you are reading the text, the **Questions/Read** section of the guide provides the questions which the text is addressing in each portion of the chapter. These questions can serve as a check to make sure you are absorbing and comprehending the information contained in the text. Its convenient outline form can also aid in note taking. By answering the questions as you read and writing the answers in your study guide, you can make sure you have a handle on all of the relevant topics in the chapter.

The **Study Skills Exercises** section provides a back end check on your retention and understanding of the material in the chapter. A careful analysis of the text should enable you to answer all of the questions in this section. It can also pinpoint areas of weakness, which could be remedied before you take any formal examinations on the material. This section includes both objective and subjective questions including map exercises and extended essay topics. The map exercises can be particularly profitable because often geography is the major force that drives the development of history. Questions concerning the chronology of events are likewise of great importance because dates and relative orderings of events create the context of history.

In summary, here is the standard outline for all Study Guide chapters:

SURVEY
> Chapter Overview
> Chapter Objectives

QUESTIONS/READ
>   Main headings of the Textbook
>   Subheadings of the Textbook
>   Chronology

STUDY SKILLS EXERCISES
The Following Will Be Included in Each Chapter: But There May Be Additional Exercises called Study Tips in the Earlier Chapters
>   Making Connections
>   Reflections
>   Vocabulary
>   Maps

RECITE/REVIEW
>   Multiple Choice
>   Short Essay
>   Extended Essay
>   Answers To Multiple Choice (with text page numbers)

PREFACE TO *OUT OF MANY*

In the Preface to the Student in this study guide, I suggest that you always read the prefaces and forewords of your textbooks to see what themes are emphasized. Your authors use the theme of community, which I will also utilize in the study guide questions. You will understand the text better if you take time to read this textbook preface and answer the following:

1. How can American history be viewed as a struggle for community?
2. What is the definition of community?
3. How has community been reinvented rather than lost?
4. What is the underlying dialectic of this book?
5. What is acculturation and what has encouraged it?
6. How do barbecues illustrate acculturation?
7. How does the Navajo experience illustrate the ideas expressed by these authors?
8. What are the ideas of John Dewey and Horace Kallen on American history and diversity?
9. What is the basic plan of this book?
10. What special features are offered in this textbook?

RECONSTRUCTION, 1863—1877

SURVEY

Chapter Overview: Reconstruction was a conflict in three areas. The first area was who was to conduct it, the executive or the legislative branch. This led to political battles between President Johnson and the Radical Republicans. The second area was between Radical Republicans and a white South that refused to be reconstructed. A third area of conflict was between blacks and whites, with the latter trying to diminish any gains of the former slaves by enacting black codes and by condoning groups such as the Ku Klux Klan. Eventually Reconstruction would fail because the Radicals lost the will to struggle and the Republican Party became more identified with business. A disputed election in 1877 ended in a compromise that allowed Hayes to take the presidency if federal troops were withdrawn from the South.

Chapter Objectives: After reading the chapter and applying the study methods recommended, you should be able to:

1. Describe the problems of community in Hale Country, Alabama as typical of the struggle in the South after the Civil War.
2. Compare the Reconstruction plans of Lincoln and Johnson to the plan of the Radical Republicans and explain how the feuding led to impeachment of President Johnson.
3. Discuss the issues of freedom for African Americans after the Civil War.
4. Summarize the problems in reconstructing the seceded states.
5. Trace the changes in the North and in the federal government away from Reconstruction and include the electoral crisis and compromise of 1876 and 1877.
6. Make connections with chapters 4, 11, 15: discuss the problems of restructuring the southern society after the Civil War and the ending of slavery in light of the historic development of the South.

QUESTIONS/READ

AMERICAN COMMUNITIES: **Hale County, Alabama: From Slavery to Freedom in a Black Belt Community:** How was this community an example of the problems faced by newly freed African Americans? What changes were made? What prompted white counterattacks? What was the response of the federal government? Identify: Union League, Ku Klux Klan, Second Reconstruction.

THE POLITICS OF RECONSTRUCTION: What were the major political issues in Reconstruction? What was and was not solved by the Civil War? What did the historical developments of the Reconstruction era revolve around?

The Defeated South: What price did the white South pay for secession, war and defeat? What share of the nation's wealth did the South hold in 1870 compared to 1860? Why did racial order increase as an issue?

Abraham Lincoln's Plan: What was Lincoln's plan for Reconstruction? What opposition did he meet and what alternative plan did they offer? As exemplified by the Wade-Davis bill, how did Radical Republicans see Reconstruction? What was the issue of land distribution and why did it not materialize? What things did Lincoln and the Radicals agree on? Identify: Proclamation of Amnesty and Reconstruction, Ten Percent Plan, Wade-Davis Bill, Butler's policy, Field Order 15, Freedmen's Bureau, Thirteenth Amendment, John Wilkes Booth.

Andrew Johnson and Presidential Reconstruction: What were Johnson's views of Reconstruction and how did this conflict with the Congress? What was Johnson's plan for Reconstruction and what goal did he have in mind? How did he hope this would translate politically? Why did his views place him on a collision course with the Radicals?

The Radical Republican Vision: What was the Radical view of Reconstruction and how did George W. Julian and Thaddeus Stevens typify it? What were "Black Codes" and what effect did they have on northern Republicans? How did these codes affect public support for the Radicals? What bills did the Radicals attempt to pass? What did Johnson do to the bills and how did he unite opposition to him? What happened in the 1866 congressional elections? Identify: Joint Committee on Reconstruction, Civil Rights Act and Freedmen's Bureau, Fourteenth Amendment, "waving the bloody shirt."

Congressional Reconstruction and the Impeachment Crisis: What was the congressional Reconstruction plan and how did Johnson react? What was the basis of the impeachment charges? What was significant about Johnson's narrow acquittal?

The Election of 1868: What were the overall results of the election of 1868? How did Johnson react after impeachment? What states were readmitted by the time of the election? What was the Republican program on black suffrage in the North? What violence occurred during the election and what effect did it have? Identify: Fifteenth Amendment.

Woman's Suffrage and Reconstruction: How was this era a turning point for woman's suffrage? What was the issue with the Fourteenth and Fifteenth Amendments? What effect did it have on women suffragists as a group? How did the views of Susan B. Anthony and Elizabeth Cady Stanton compare to Lucy Stone and Frederick Douglass? While not gaining the vote, what did women accomplish for their cause? Identify: Equal Rights Association, American Woman Suffrage Association, National Woman Suffrage Association.

THE MEANING OF FREEDOM: What did freedom mean to African Americans after the war? How did they carry it out?

Moving About: Why was moving about a major test of freedom for African Americans? Where did many of them go? How did many planters react?

The African American Family: How did emancipation affect the family ties of former slaves? How was it part of the definition of freedom? How were gender roles affected by emancipation?

African American Churches and Schools: What developments took place in African American churches and schools during post-emancipation years? Why was the church particularly significant as an institution to African Americans? Which denominations were the most popular? What types of schools and teachers were available? What was the level of literacy? Identify: wayside schools, AMA, Tougaloo-Hampton-Fisk.

Labor and Land after Slavery: What type of laboring and farming system replaced the old plantation system? What did many African Americans try to do and how were they thwarted? What was the sharecropping system? How widespread did sharecropping become? Identify: "forty acres and a mule."

The Origins of African American Politics: What political activities were begun by freed blacks? Where were these activities the most common? What were the issues discussed at the statewide conventions in 1865 and 1866? Identify: North Carolina Freedmen's Convention, First Reconstruction Act, Union League.

SOUTHERN POLITICS AND SOCIETY: What had the Republicans hoped to do in the South and what actually occurred? How did Democrats regain control by 1877?

Southern Republicans: What groups made up the coalition of Republican support in the postwar South? In which states did they have the most influence? Identify: carpetbaggers, scalawags, "confiscation radicals."

Reconstructing the States: A Mixed Record: Why was the reconstruction of the southern states a mixed record? Who dominated the southern constitutional conventions and what types of documents did they produce? What segregation was there and why? What patterns of discrimination persisted? What was the "gospel of prosperity" and what was accomplished under it?

White Resistance and "Redemption": What was the extent of white resistance and how did they gain "redemption?" Why was there no real two-party system in the South during Reconstruction? What violence developed and what did the federal government do about it? Why did this intervention eventually fade away? How did Supreme Court rulings curtail federal attempts to protect African American rights? Identify: Ku Klux Klan Act, "redeemed States," Slaughterhouse cases, *U.S. v. Reese*, *U.S. v. Cruikshank*, Civil Rights Cases.

"King Cotton" and the Crop Lien System: How did the southern social system work to reinforce dependence on cotton and the crop lien system? What problems and repercussions were caused by this? What was the wealth per capita in the South compared to other sections of the country by the 1890s? How many whites and blacks were sharecroppers or tenant farmers by 1880?

RECONSTRUCTING THE NORTH: What "reconstruction" took place in the North? As expressed by Abraham Lincoln, what economic views did the North think were superior? What problems developed in the economy and how did the Republicans respond to them?

The Age of Capital: What were the characteristics of the Age of Capital? How much had industrial production and the proportion of nonagricultural workers grown over 1865? What world position was the U.S. in at the manufacturing level? What was the place of the railroads in the Age of Capital and what effects did railroad construction have? What other industries boomed? Identify: Promontory Point, Pennsylvania Railroad, Cornelius Vanderbilt, Credit Mobilier, National Mineral Act of 1866, Standard Oil.

Liberal Republicans and the Election of 1872: Who were the Liberal Republicans and what did they believe? What was their view of Reconstruction? What did the Election of 1872 illustrate? What eventually happened to the Liberal Republicans? Identify: Tweed Ring, Charles Francis Adams, "Root, Hog, or Die," Horace Greeley.

The Depression of 1873: What was the extent of the panic of 1873? What caused it and how significant was it? As stated by E.L. Godkin, what was the attitude of many toward any government role in alleviating hardships from the panic? What effect did the panic have on the old free-labor ideology? Identify: "tramp," Chicago Citizens' Association.

The Electoral Crisis of 1876: What happened in the 1876 election to precipitate a crisis? Who was Samuel J. Tilden and what platform did he run on? Who was Rutherford B. Hayes and what was his platform? What did Congress do to try to settle the electoral deadlock? What did the electoral commission do and how was the crisis solved? What was the "Compromise of 1877?" Identify: Whiskey Ring, home rule.

CONCLUSION: In what sense did Reconstruction succeed and in what way did it fail? What was the "Second Reconstruction?" What shift occurred in the government as a protector? What question replaced the "southern question?"

CHRONOLOGY: What time span is being covered? What is the significance of this particular time span? What are the major events covered in this chapter? How do they connect to the chapter title? Who are the significant people as groups or as individuals involved in these events? What are the significant places? What important concepts are connected to these events?

STUDY SKILLS EXERCISES

1. Reflection: Imagine yourself a teacher in the Freedmen's Bureau. What would you have thought you could contribute to Reconstruction?
2. Making Connections: To what extent did both North and South continue the economic divisions and sectionalism of the antebellum period in the postwar period?

3. Vocabulary:

antebellum, p. 484	integrated, p. 500
centralization, p. 488	incendiary, p. 501
obstructionism, p. 489	panic, p. 506
denominations, p. 494	

4. Maps:
   a. *Reconstruction of the South, 1866-1877:* (p. 489) What types of districts were established in 1867 in the South? What southern state was first to be readmitted and also have the Democrats returned to power?
   b. *The Barrow Plantation, Oglethorpe County, Georgia, 1860 and 1881:* (p. 496) What changes are evident from 1860 to 1881 due to emancipation?
   c. *Southern Sharecropping, 1880:* (p. 503) Which areas and states had the most sharecropping arrangements?
   d. *The Election of 1876:* (p. 509) Which states had disputed votes?

RECITE/REVIEW

MULTIPLE CHOICE:

1. The freed African Americans represented what fraction of the total southern population?
   a. one-tenth
   b. one-fourth
   c. one-third
   d. one-half

2. Lincoln's Proclamation of Amnesty and Reconstruction was called the Ten Percent Plan. This number referred to the percentage of
   a. southerners swearing loyalty to the Constitution.
   b. blacks who would be allowed to vote.
   c. lands redistributed to blacks on a homestead basis.
   d. Republican party members in each reconstructed state.

3. Both Lincoln and Johnson shared the view that Reconstruction
   a. should punish the South for secession.
   b. was a presidential function.
   c. needed to be a complete socio-economic transformation.
   d. prohibited any real conciliation of North and South.

4. Which one of the following is the RESULT of the other three?
   a. President Johnson impeached
   b. Tenure of Office Act passed
   c. Civil Rights Act passed
   d. Reconstruction Acts passed

5. By 1880 nearly three-quarters of black southerners became
   a. Democrats.
   b. factory workers.
   c. "redeemers."
   d. sharecroppers.

6. Which one of the following is NOT one of the three groups that made up the fledgling Republican coalition in the postwar South?
   a. African Americans
   b. Radical Democrats
   c. white Northerners
   d. prewar Whigs

7. If you lived in eastern Tennessee, western North Carolina, or northern Alabama, and were a small farmer, you were most likely to be in a group derisively called
   a. tramps.
   c. carpetbaggers.
   b. redemptioners.
   d. scalawags.

8. In the southern state constitutional conventions called under the First Reconstruction Act, the largest majority of delegates were
   a. southern white Republicans.
   c. newly freed African Americans.
   b. northern white Republicans.
   d. antebellum free African Americans.

9. Which one of the following Supreme Court cases is not correctly paired with the amendment or law that it limited?
   a. Slaughterhouse Cases/Fourteenth Amendment
   b. *U.S. v. Reese*/Ku Klux Klan Act
   c. *U.S. v. Cruikshank*/Fifteenth Amendment
   d. Civil Rights Cases/Thirteenth Amendment

10. In 1877, the same year that federal troops were withdrawn from the South, they were used in the North to
    a. repress Ku Klux Klan sympathizers.
    b. restore control after a race riot in New York City.
    c. break a violent national railroad strike.
    d. drive any remaining eastern Indians to western reservations.

11. The first big businesses in America were the
    a. mining companies.
    c. railroad companies.
    b. oil companies.
    d. steel mills.

12. Which one of the following has the LEAST in common with the other three?
    a. Credit Mobilier
    c. Whiskey Ring
    b. Tweed Ring
    d. Confiscation Radicals

13. The Chicago Citizen's Association had the MOST in common with
    a. E.L. Godkin and Horace Greeley.
    b. Andrew Johnson and Edwin Stanton.
    c. New York labor leaders and workers.
    d. Orville Babcock and William W. Belknap.

14. Which one of the following is the RESULT of the other three?
    a. Electoral Commission elects Hayes president
    b. Election between Tilden and Hayes disputed
    c. Federal troops withdrawn from the South
    d. Compromise of 1877

CHRONOLOGY AND MAP QUESTIONS:

15. Which one of the following events is NOT correctly matched to the year in which it took place?
    a. Thirteenth Amendment ratified/1865
    b. Ku Klux Klan Act passed/1868
    c. Fifteenth Amendment ratified/1870
    d. Slaughterhouse Cases/1873

16. The Union and Central Pacific met at Promontory Point in Utah Territory in
    a. 1866.   c. 1872.
    b. 1869.   d. 1877.

17. The first southern state to be readmitted and the Democrats returned to power was
    a. Tennessee.   c. Texas.
    b. Florida.   d. Georgia.

18. Which one of the following was NOT a state in which sharecropping became most pervasive?
    a. Georgia   c. Texas
    b. Alabama   d. North Carolina

SHORT ESSAY:

19. What role did the railroads play in the settlement of the West?

20. In what ways does Boss Tweed represent urban politics during this period?

21. Why did many politicians oppose universal suffrage?

EXTENDED ESSAY:

22. Why did black leaders not fight for integrated public schools during this period?

23. Discuss the factors leading to President Johnson's impeachment.

24. Discuss the meaning of freedom for African Americans of this period. Was the freedom a real freedom, or was it freedom in name only?

ANSWERS-CHAPTER 17

MULTIPLE CHOICE:
1.	c, p. 482	6.	b, pp. 498-499	11.	c, p. 505
2.	a, p. 485	7.	d, p. 499	12.	d, pp. 487, 506-508
3.	b, pp. 485-486	8.	a, p. 499	13.	a, p. 508
4.	a, pp. 488-489	9.	d, p. 502	14.	c, pp. 508-509
5.	d, p. 497	10.	c, p. 509		

CHRONOLOGY AND MAPS:
15.	b, p. 510	17.	a, p. 489
16.	b, p. 510	18.	d, p. 503

SHORT ESSAY:
19-21

EXTENDED ESSAY:
22-24

CONQUEST AND SURVIVAL: THE TRANS-MISSISSIPPI WEST, 1860—1900

SURVEY

Chapter Overview: If you skipped the first section of this study guide, please read the Preface to the Student before starting this section. This study guide is based on a particular study method and you will get more out of it if you read the explanatory material as well as the Preface to your textbook.

This chapter covers the changes in transportation and technology that enabled white settlers to move into the trans-Mississippi West, an area viewed earlier as the Great American Desert and occupied by Indians and Mexicans. Mining, commercial farming and ranching brought in more settlers as homestead laws and railroad land advertising promoted the settlement of the Great Plains. Indian communities were under siege and the Indians generally were pushed onto reservations. As the primitive West disappeared, parts of it were preserved in national parks, in paintings, written works, and photography as well as in a stereotyped Wild West. Indian cultures were seriously affected by the Dawes Act but they managed to endure and rejuvenate.

Chapter Objectives: After reading this chapter and following the study suggestions given, you should be able to:

1. Explain how the Oklahoma Land Rush illustrated the effects on old and new communities in the trans-Mississippi West.
2. Describe the impact on and transformation of the Indian communities in the trans-Mississippi West.
3. Discuss the West as an internal empire including the role of the federal government in its acquisition.
4. Summarize the impact of settlement on existing communities as well as the creation of new ones.
5. Outline the agricultural changes from the Plains to cattle industry to California including effects on the Midwest and East.
6. Summarize the efforts to create images of the primitive West in writings, paintings, photography, natural parks, and in stereotyped images of the Wild West.

QUESTIONS/READ

AMERICAN COMMUNITIES: **The Oklahoma Land Rush:** What was the Oklahoma Land Rush and what effect did it have on community? What was the Indian Territory and how did it come to be open to settlement? How did the Indians fare before and after the Civil War? Identify: Five Civilized Tribes, No Man's Land, "Boomers," "Soddies," Curtis Act.

INDIAN PEOPLES UNDER SIEGE: What Indian peoples were there in the West and how did they react to increasing white settlement? What ultimately happened to most Indian communities?

> **On the Eve of Conquest:** What Indian peoples populated the West and what were their locations? What effects did European conquest have? How were many tribes protected until after the Civil War? What was the population? How did Indians adapt to changing conditions? What was the history of federal Indian policy? What was Indian Territory and why did the idea not survive? Identify: *Cherokee v. Georgia.*
>
> **Reservations and the Slaughter of the Buffalo:** What was the reservation policy? What was it designed to do? What actually happened to the various tribes? Why were the buffalo slaughtered and what effect did it have on tribes? Identify: Isaac Stevens, Medicine Lodge Treaty of 1867, Lakota, vision seekers.
>
> **The Indian Wars:** Why did the tribes become involved in various wars and what was the eventual result? Which tribes were most involved? What was the extent of actual resistance? Identify: Black Kettle, Sand Creek Massacre, Bozeman Trail, Great Sioux War, Red Cloud, Treaty of Fort Laramie, W.T. Sherman, Crazy Horse, Sitting Bull, George Custer, Little Bighorn, Greasy Grass, *Paha Sapa,* Cochise, Geronimo, Red River War.
>
> **The Nez Percé:** Who were the Nez Percé and what was their experience with conquest? What changed Indian-white relations in this situation? How did the Nez Percé respond? What did Chief Joseph try to do? What eventually happened to him and his people? Identify: Chief Tukekas, Chief Joseph, Wallowa.

THE INTERNAL EMPIRE: What was the internal empire and how was it acquired? How were earlier communities affected?

> **Mining Communities:** What types of communities and settlement patterns were typical in mining areas? What effect did mining have on westward expansion? What type of labor union structure developed and how successful was it? What ethnic groups did unions generally represent? What effect did mining have on the environment? Identify: Comstock Lode, Anaconda Copper Mining Company, Virginia City, Butte, "Helldorados," Caminetti Act.
>
> **Mormon Settlements:** Who were the Mormons and how significant were they to the agricultural settling of the West? How did they structure their community and their agriculture? What brought them into conflict with the federal government? What was the result? How was their way of life changed? Identify: Joseph Smith, Brigham Young, Deseret, Utah Territory, *United States v. Reynolds,* Edmunds Act, Edmunds-Tucker Act.
>
> **The Southwest:** What new settlement occurred in the Southwest and how did that affect existing communities? How did the United States acquire the territory? What type of economic and social zone developed? How were different Mexican populations affected? Identify: Gadsden Purchase, Treaty of Guadalupe Hidalgo, Sante Fe Ring, Estevan Ochoa,

10

Amadors, Juan Cortina, *Cortina's War,* Las Corras Blancas, Los Alianzo Hispano-American, *Mutualistes,* Cinco de Mayo.

THE CATTLE INDUSTRY: Why did the cattle industry develop when it did and how successful was it? Identify: Joseph McCoy, Jesse Chisholm.

Cowboys: Who were cowboys as workers and as organized laborers? What was the reality of work for a cowboy? What was the variety of ethnic origin among cowboys? What type of experiences did various ethnic groups bring to the cattle industry?

Cowgirls and Prostitutes: Who were the majority of women that managed ranches or worked in the cattle industry? How prevalent was prostitution in the West? How did racial ranking affect prostitution? What was the fate of most prostitutes?

Community and Conflict on the Range: What conflicts prevented the development of stable communities on the range? How violent was the West and what were the causes of the violence? How did the weather increase conflict? What caused the decline of the cattle barons? Identify: Wyatt Earp, range wars.

FARMING COMMUNITIES ON THE PLAINS: How did farming the Plains become possible? How did early explorers see the Great Plains?

The Homestead Act: What was the Homestead Act? What did its promoters hope to accomplish? Where was the Act most and least successful? What groups gained the most? What was Horace Greeley's advice? Why was it wrong?

Populating the Plains: What technology allowed the rapid populating of the Plains? What immigrant groups populated the Plains? What types of communities did they establish? How high was mobility? What exclusive hierarchies and clubs existed? Identify: Hutterites, Oddfellows-Elks-Templars, Eastern Star-Companions of the Forest.

Work, Dawn to Dusk: What types of work did farm families engage in on a daily basis? What cooperative efforts were there among families, friends, and neighbors? How did the cash economy affect the farm families? What happened to many small family farms? Identify: one room school.

THE WORLD'S BREADBASKET: How did the farmlands of America become the world's breadbasket? What new technologies allowed this? What were the effects?

New Production Technologies: What were the new technologies that affected agricultural production? What were the statistics of increased production with technological improvements? What scientific supports were available to farmers? What problems occurred in spite of technology and scientific knowledge? Identify: John Deere, Cyrus McCormick, Morrill Act of 1862, Department of Agriculture, Weather Bureau, Hatch Act of 1887, 98th meridian.

Producing for the Market: How did producing for the market affect farmers and farm families? What crop was most productive? How was Oliver Dalrymple an example of a successful farmer?

California: Why was California particularly significant in terms of farming trends? Why was California the model for agribusiness? What crops were the basis of farmer success in California? What were Sunkist, Paul Masson and Sun Maid symbolic of?

The Toll on the Land: What was the toll on the land? What types of problems developed? Identify: Timber Culture Act, National Reclamation Act, Lake Tulare, Forest Service, General Land Revision Act of 1891, Forest Management Act.

The Western Landscape: What was the significance of the western region and its people to Americans in general?

Nature's Majesty: How did the majesty of the western landscape get publicized in the East? What significant areas were set aside as preserves and parks? Identify: William H. Jackson, Thomas Moran, Yellowstone, Alfred Bierstadt.

The Legendary Wild West: What was the essence of the Wild West as a legend and how was it promoted? How did Theodore Roosevelt promote the imagery of the West? Who was Edward Zane Carroll Judson and what was his significance in promoting the Wild West? Identify: dime novels, Nat Love, Deadwood Dick, Calamity Jane, Joseph McCoy, William F. Cody, Owen Wister's The Virginian.

The "American Primitive:" What images of the West were promoted in the "American Primitive?" What effect did they have on Native American study? Identify: Charles Schreyvogel, Charles Russell, Frederic Remington, Edward Sheriff Curtis, Lewis Henry Morgan, Alice Cunningham Fletcher, Suzette La Flesche, Boy and Girl Scouts.

THE TRANSFORMATION OF INDIAN SOCIETIES: How were Indian societies transformed?

Reform Policy and Politics: What was the aim of reform policies and how were they carried out? Who was Helen Hunt Jackson and what effect did she have? What was the Dawes Severalty Act? What was its intent and actual results to Indian communities and reservation land? What act reversed the Dawes Act? Identify: A Century of Dishonor, Indian Rights Association, WNIA.

The Ghost Dance: What was the origin and intent of the Ghost Dance? How did many whites react to the Ghost Dance? Identify: Wovoka, Wounded Knee Creek, Big Foot, Black Elk.

Endurance and Rejuvenation: How did various Indian tribes survive and rejuvenate? How did those who did adapt and cooperate with whites fare? How did the Navajo and Hopi survive? Identify: Pimas, Yanas, Flatheads, Quapaws, Cheyennes, "Dine," "Long Walk," potlatch.

CONCLUSION: What did the transformation of the trans-Mississippi West mean for America?

CHRONOLOGY: What time span is being covered? What is the significance of this particular time span? What are the major events covered in this chapter? How do they connect to the chapter title? Who are the significant people as groups or as individuals involved in these events? What are the significant places? What important terms and concepts are connected to these events?

NOTE: Since these questions are always the same, they will not be repeated after this chapter. I will just remind you to use these standard questions.

STUDY SKILLS EXERCISES

1. Study Tip: In the preface of this guide, the skill of identification was mentioned as a useful way to study history. Use the pattern of who or what, when, where, why in identifying major items. You can put these terms on 3x5 cards or use the Cornell method. Be sure to incorporate any pertinent material from illustrations or maps. It may also be useful to blend in material from various parts of the chapter or chapters. Do not expect all relevant material to be in one place. Try this with the Dawes Severalty Act on pp. 540-542 and see how your answer compares to the item below. Note that I left out the how but if your professor has numerous essay questions, the how might be included.

    Dawes Severalty Act
    Who or What: a law passed by Congress
    When: 1887-policy until 1934
    Where: to cover Indians on reservation lands
    Why: to break up tribes by giving land to individual Indians in order to force them to assimilate to white culture and become citizens. Reformers mistakenly hoped it would help but it undermined tribal culture and resulted in a 60% loss of reservation lands and 66% loss of individual allotments.

    If your professor asks you to write short identification answers on a test, you should take the above information and blend it into a smooth paragraph as you write it out.

2. Reflection is one of the six Rs in the study method described in the preface. Doing this will enrich your understanding of the material and involve you actively in the text. For example:
    a. Imagine yourself as an immigrant traveling west by train and settling. What would you write to your relatives back home about your trip?
    b. Imagine yourself as a Native American or Mexican overhearing a Fourth of July speaker praising the American farmer for winning and settling an empty untamed West. How would you reply?
    c. Consider all the various stereotyped images of the West you have gained from books, television or movies. How would you revise those images after reading this chapter?

3. Remember to pay attention to maps, graphs and illustrations. They can give you context and cues to understand and remember the material. For example, in this chapter when you read about increased productivity of the farmer, you should also look at the chart on p. 556 labeled "Hand v. Machine Labor on the Farm." What conclusions can you draw from it in relation to the text?

4. Making Connections: In the preface, I mentioned reducing and rearranging information. One way to do this is to make a chart. A chart helps you compare and connect information. There are major advantages to doing this. First, you have elements of the entire chapter in a compact form to which you can add relevant lecture information. The second advantage is that doing a chart reinforces the material either for objective or essay exams. The third is that you are actively involved in the material as you construct your

charts. You can see the connections between things. I have put an example of a chart for you at the end of this chapter. Be alert to others that you can develop. You should have brief phrases or terms that remind you of the subject. Remember that your goal is summary. DO NOT try to cram everything from the chapter onto the chart. Then you can quickly review. Put page numbers after your phrases so that you can very quickly look back to refresh your memory on an item.

5. Vocabulary:

assimilation, p. 516	intrinsic, p. 528
nomadic, p. 518	coffer, p. 531
sabotaged, p. 523	lampooned, p. 537
cohesion, p. 524	eradicate, p. 540
bonanza, p. 526	tenacious, p. 542

6. Maps: If you are not quickly familiar with the locations of the western states, use one of the blank maps at the back of this study guide to practice naming them. The text authors assume you are geographically literate. If your professor has map tests, there are a variety of blank practice maps for you to photocopy at the end of the study guide.
   a. *Oklahoma Territory:* (p. 515) What variety of Indian tribes were in Oklahoma Territory? What areas were affected by the land runs?
   b. *Major Indian Battles and Indian Reservations, 1860-1900:* (p. 517) Locate the Indian Tribes and battles referred to in the text. What was the result for Indian and white populations?
   c. *Mormon Cultural Diffusion:* (p. 524) What areas of the West were permeated by Mormon settlements?
   d. *The Establishment of National Parks and Forests:* (p. 536) Compare the relative size of national parks and forests east and west of the Mississippi. What was the earliest national park; national forest?
   e. As a way of context and review, be able to label all the states west of the Mississippi.

RECITE/REVIEW

MULTIPLE CHOICE:

1. Which one of the following groups was NOT part of the pressure to reduce and reorganize the Indian Territory of the Five Civilized Tribes?
   a. other Indian groups
   b. boomers
   c. miners
   d. African Americans

2. This act dissolved Indian Territory and sovereign status which the Five Tribes did not regain until 1977:
   a. Curtis Act.
   b. Morrill Act.
   c. Dawes Act.
   d. Caminetti Act.

3. At the close of the Civil War, the majority of Indians in the trans-Mississippi West lived in
   a. the Southwest.
   c. the Great Plains.
   b. Texas.
   d. Indian Territory.

4. As an example of settler pressure, this part of Indian Territory was abolished and opened to white settlement in 1854:
   a. Kansas and Nebraska
   c. No Man's Land
   b. North and South Dakota
   d. the Southwest

5. The reformers' intentions in both the reservation policy and the Dawes Act was to
   a. protect Indian culture.
   c. assimilate tribes into white culture.
   b. curtail white settlement.
   d. get tribes to fight each other.

6. The destruction of the buffalo and their way of life convinced many of these vision seeking Great Plains people to conclude they could only fight or die:
   a. Comanche
   c. Apache
   b. Navajo
   d. Lakota

7. "The more we can kill this year, the less will have to be killed next year" was an example of the harshness of Indian-white relations as stated by
   a. George Armstrong Custer.
   c. Geronimo.
   b. Wovoka.
   d. William Tecumseh Sherman.

8. Which one of the following has the LEAST to do with the others?
   a. *United States v. Reynolds*
   c. Deseret
   b. Sante Fe Ring
   d. Brigham Young

9. The Mormons learned how to survive in their area by relying on farming techniques learned from
   a. local Indian tribes.
   b. the newly-created Department of Agriculture.
   c. African Americans whose ancestors practiced it as an age-old art.
   d. Spanish priests.

10. The "Cortina War" is a good example of conflict over western expansion between
   a. open range ranchers and crop farmers who wanted fencing.
   b. striking miners and their employers.
   c. Mexican communities and Anglo farmer encroachment.
   d. California ranchers fighting each other over water rights.

11. Which one of the following was NOT a reason for the demise of the huge cattle barons by the late 1880s?
   a. overstocked herds that depleted the limited grass supply
   b. constant danger of Indian attack
   c. severe summer and winter weather in 1885-87
   d. pressure to fence and regulate formerly open land

12. Which one of the following is NOT true of the Homestead Act of 1862?
    a. It was most successful in the central and upper Midwest.
    b. Big-time land speculators gained the most.
    c. A person could gain land by settling and improving it over five years.
    d. Most farmers gained their lands this way.

13. Technological improvements allowed the average farmer to produce up to THIS many more times than before:
    a. two
    c. twenty-five
    b. ten
    d. fifty

14. From Nebraska to California, this became the most prosperous crop in the late 1800s:
    a. livestock
    c. corn
    b. cotton
    d. wheat

15. These two people who were actual westerners staged and popularized the Wild West Show:
    a. Edward Zane Carroll Judson and Owen Wister
    b. Nat Love and Calamity Jane
    c. Frederic Remington and Charles Russell
    d. Joseph McCoy and William Cody

16. Which one of the following is NOT one of the accomplishments of Alice Cunningham Fletcher?
    a. She wrote the critical work, *Century of Dishonor*.
    b. She helped support the Omaha Indians.
    c. She wrote a study on the status of Indian peoples.
    d. She was a pioneering ethnographer in studying Indian societies.

17. Which one of the following was the RESULT of the other three?
    a. Great Sioux War
    c. popularity of the Ghost Dance
    b. massacre at Wounded Knee
    d. Wovoka's vision

18. The Yahi are to California as the Flatheads are to
    a. Washington.
    c. North Dakota.
    b. Arizona.
    d. Montana.

CHRONOLOGY AND MAP QUESTIONS:

19. Which one of the following gives the correct chronological order of these events?
    (1) Forest Management Act   (3) Timber Culture Act
    (2) Morrill Act   (4) Dawes Severalty Act
    a. 2,3,4,1   c. 4,2,3,1
    b. 3,2,4,1   d. 1,2,4,3

20. The Census Bureau announced that the end of the frontier line happened in this year:
    a. 1870
    b. 1880
    c. 1890
    d. 1900

21. Which one of the following events did NOT occur in 1866?
    a. Texas cattle drives begin.
    b. The reservation system is established in Medicine Lodge Treaty.
    c. Alaska is purchased.
    d. Yellowstone National Park is created.

22. No Man's Land was located in
    a. western Oklahoma.
    b. eastern Dakotas.
    c. northern Kansas.
    d. central Wyoming.

23. The conflict known as Greasy Grass or Little Bighorn took place in
    a. Wyoming.
    b. Montana.
    c. South Dakota.
    d. Nebraska.

24. Which one of the following is NOT a Great Plains state?
    a. Montana
    b. North Dakota
    c. Wyoming
    d. Utah

25. In 1872 the first national park was established in
    a. Grand Canyon.
    b. Sequoia.
    c. Yellowstone.
    d. Yosemite.

SHORT ESSAY:

26. Discuss how, in a sense, "Custer's Last Stand" was really a defeat for the Indians.

27. Contrast the image presented in the Wild West shows with the reality of life in the western frontier times.

28. Describe the relationships between the Indians and the various American religious groups during this time period.

EXTENDED ESSAY:

29. In what ways did the railroad change the lives and the habits of Midwesterners?

30. What role did technology play in the evolution of farming from a family-based, labor-intensive activity into agribusiness?

31. What effects did settlers have on the natural landscape of the West, and what effects did the natural landscape have on the settlers?

ANSWERS-CHAPTER 18

MULTIPLE CHOICE:
1.	c, pp. 514-5	10.	c, p. 525
2.	a, p. 515	11.	b, p. 528
3.	c, p. 516	12.	d, p. 529
4.	a, p. 517	13.	b, p. 533
5.	c, p. 517	14.	d, p. 534
6.	d, p. 518	15.	d, p. 538
7.	d, p. 520	16.	a, p. 539
8.	b, pp. 523-5	17.	b, p. 541
9.	a, p. 523	18.	d, p. 542

CHRONOLOGY AND MAP QUESTIONS:
19.	a, p. 543	23.	b, p. 517
20.	c, p. 543	24.	d, p. 528
21.	d, p. 543	25.	c, p. 536
22.	a, p. 515		

SHORT ESSAY: 26-28   EXTENDED ESSAY: 29-31

Technology and Environment	
Technology That Allowed "Conquest" of the Area	Environmental Impact of Settlement And Technologies Used*
Mining	
Cattle Ranching	
Agriculture:	
a. Central & Upper Mid-West	
b. Great Plains	
c. California	

* Include any laws that were significant in either a positive or negative way

THE INCORPORATION OF AMERICA, 1865—1900

SURVEY

Chapter Overview: This chapter covers the industrialization of America from 1865 to 1900. This transformation was based on the railroads, which in turn encouraged other industries as well as the development of large-scale corporations. Labor unions organized on a national level to counter the size and power of the employers but with mixed results. America also continued to urbanize with rapid growth of the cities unplanned and residential patterns reflecting social class divisions. The South tried to participate in the growth as the New South but generally reinforced old patterns. Gospels of wealth and work reinforced differences between the rising middle class and the factory workers but leisure time activities such as sports added to national identity.

Chapter Objectives: After reading the chapter and following the study suggestions given, you should be able to:

1. Describe the rapid industrialization and large-scale business organizations that characterized the economy as well as the gospel of wealth ideology that supported it.
2. Discuss the effects that dramatic economic change had on labor and labor organizations.
3. Outline the explosive growth of the cities as the economy expanded including the various problems that developed from concentration of the population.
4. Explain the concept of the New South and why it did not materialize except in the Piedmont communities.
5. Summarize the interests and issues in society and culture in the Gilded Age.
6. Discuss how new leisure time helped build a greater sense of national identity and at the same time created more conflicts over control of parks and recreation areas.
7. Summarize how the industrialization and urbanization of America affected community and use Chicago, Illinois as a specific example of these changes.
8. Making Connections: Chapters Eighteen and Nineteen: How did the conquest of the West prepare the way for the industrial age?

QUESTIONS/READ

AMERICAN COMMUNITIES: **Packingtown, Chicago, Illinois:** What was Packingtown and how is it an example of the changes in community in industrialized America? What local institution bridged different ethnic groups? How was Packingtown connected to the economy of the nation? What allowed the meatpacking monopoly to develop? Identify: knife men, feedlots.

THE RISE OF INDUSTRY, THE TRIUMPH OF BUSINESS: What was the extent of the rise of industry and the triumph of business?

> **A Revolution in Technology:** What was the revolution in technology? How did Thomas Alva Edison typify the revolution? What business was the major force behind economic growth and the first big business for the United States? What were the changes in the geographic centers of manufacturing, flour milling, agricultural equipment and wiring? What others would be added? What were the statistics of industrial growth? Identify: Centennial Exposition of 1876.
>
> **Mechanization Takes Command:** How did mechanized production affect all aspects of productivity? What other types of factors were important? What fuel was most significant? Where did the production line idea originate? What industries were affected by mechanized continuous production?
>
> **The Expanding Market for Goods:** How was the expanding market developed? Who were the significant mail order houses, chain stores, department stores and advertising that were part of sales and distribution?
>
> **Integration, Combination, and Merger:** What were the major methods of growth in business? Which individuals and/or companies were major examples of each? What were the causes of this large scale of operation? Identify: vertical integration, horizontal combination, Sherman Antitrust Act.
>
> **The Gospel of Wealth:** What were the basic tenets of the gospel of wealth? How did Jay Gould and Andrew Carnegie illustrate different aspects of this gospel? What was the notion of social Darwinism and who seemed to fulfill its lessons the best? Identify: Horatio Alger.

LABOR IN THE AGE OF BIG BUSINESS: How did labor and labor organizations respond to the enormous change of scale in business? What was the gospel of work? How did the gospel of work compare to the gospel of wealth? Identify: George McNeil.

> **The Changing Status of Labor:** How did the work force change? What were the statistics of change? Where did the people come from to fill the need for labor in new industries? What did a 1910 report on twenty-one industries show? How did the accelerating growth of industry shape the pool of wageworkers? How were the following workers affected: craft workers, women, African Americans, Chinese? What hazards were in the workplace? What boom and bust cycles occurred and how did that affect workers? What major depressions and minor recessions occurred? In 1883, how many industrial workers lived below the poverty line? Identify: Frederick Winslow Taylor, greenhands, outwork, Chinese Exclusion Act.
>
> **Mobilization Against the Wage System:** How did labor mobilize against the wage system? What types of views were reflected in the different organizations? How did Sylvis's National Labor Union compare to Powderly's Knights of Labor? What were the

eight-hour leagues and what did they accomplish? What was the Haymarket Square incident and how did that affect labor organizations? Identify: ladies assemblies, Leonora Barry.

The American Federation of Labor: What was the American Federation of Labor and what differentiated it from the earlier NLU or Knights? What groups did the AFL concentrate on organizing? How successful were they? Identify: Samuel Gompers, Labor Day.

THE INDUSTRIAL CITY: How did the new industrialization compare to the older manufacturing before the Civil War? What were the successes and problems of the industrial city? Where did most manufacturing take place?

Populating the City: How fast did the population grow in the cities and what types of groups made up the total? How many Americans lived in cities by 1890? Did all immigrants intend to stay in America? Which immigrant groups had the most experience with urban life? Where did different ethnic groups settle?

The Urban Landscape: How was the urban landscape developed? What effects did social class have on the structures of cities? How did mass transportation affect cities? Identify: dumbbell, Fifth Avenue and other wealthy neighborhoods, Frederick Law Olmsted, Louis H. Sullivan, American Renaissance, John Roebling, suburbs.

The City and the Environment: How did technological changes in cities affect the environment? What variety of environmental problems did cities face? How successful were they in dealing with them? Identify: buffer zones.

THE NEW SOUTH: What was the idea of the New South and how successful was it? How did the South compare to the North in the industrial boom? What types of things held the South back?

Industrialization: What advantages did the South have for industrialization? What was Henry Woodfin Grady's vision of a "New South?" What problems between North and South are illustrated by the Birmingham steel industry and the cotton mills? What were the extractive industries of the South?

Southern Labor: How did Reconstruction and its demise affect southern labor? How were various groups of laborers affected? How did organized labor fare in the South? How did southern wages and traditions affect working? Identify: Red Shirts, Ellison Smyth, convict labor, good roads movement.

Transformation of Piedmont Communities: Where were the Piedmont communities and how were they transformed by the New South? What type of community was found in a company town or mill village? What were customs of incorporation ?

CULTURE AND SOCIETY IN THE GILDED AGE: How did culture and society develop in the Gilded Age? What differences were there in levels of wealth? Who coined the time period as "Gilded Age?"

Conspicuous Consumption: What was "conspicuous consumption" and who coined the phrase? What are some examples? What was significant about Newport as well as New York's Waldorf-Astoria hotel? What changes took place in the arts? Identify: "Diamond Jim" Brady, H.H. Richardson, Carnegie.

Gentility and the Middle Class: What was the new middle class that developed? How did they attempt to establish social status? How did changes in household technology affect women's roles? What was "culture" to the middle class? What items established status? What changes occurred for middle class children? Identify: Harriet Spofford's *Art Decoration,* Chautauqua, gospel of exercise, *The Brownie Book, St. Nicholas, Little Women.*

Life in the Streets: What was life like for new immigrants and working class people in general? What is the common element of the terms *Malbuerica, Ama Reka,* and *Dollerica?* What types of communities did newcomers seek? Where were many forced to reside? How were working class women and children affected? What markets were created by the buying power of the working class? Identify: *barrios,* Young Men's and Young Women's Christian Associations, Tin Pan Alley, ragtime, Coney Island.

CULTURES IN CONFLICT, CULTURE IN COMMON: What cultures were in conflict? What common culture was being developed?

Education: What caused the rapid expansion of education? What level was considered free by the end of the nineteenth century? What areas of education expanded and what groups did they serve? How did education differ based on gender, race and/or social class? Identify: kindergarten, Morrill Act, Johns Hopkins, Vassar, Women's Educational and Industrial Union, industrial education, Fisk, Booker T. Washington, Tuskegee.

Leisure and Public Space: What class differences were apparent on the question of control of public space and the leisure pursuits to be followed in them? What is the Forest Park/Tandy Park issue in St. Louis an example of? Identify: blue laws.

National Pastimes: What types of activities became popular pastimes for young people of both middle and working classes? Identify: Scott Joplin, vaudeville, National pastime, Knickerbockers, National League, Albert Spaulding, Negro Leagues, Brotherhood of Professional Baseball Players, home team.

CONCLUSION: How had industrialization and urbanization opened new worlds for rich and poor alike? What class problems remained?

CHRONOLOGY: Apply the standard questions from p.11 of the Study Guide.

STUDY SKILLS EXERCISES

1. Imagine yourself as a person from a rural area coming to the city to find a job. What obstacles might you find and what possible successes would you have? Repeat this reflection as an African American and as a newly arrived immigrant from Eastern Europe.

2. When you look at each beginning question in the heading and subheading under the QUESTIONS/READ section, remember that you cannot immediately answer the questions. You need to read the total section and/or subsection to answer them adequately. Do not be content with saying yes or no as an answer. You should imagine that you are explaining the answers to someone else. This forces you to consider how you would arrange your answers and what clarifying examples and illustrations you would use.

3. Look at the chapter outline on p. 548. Remember to make the arrangement of a textbook work for you. At the very minimum, you should be able to recognize or identify every term or name in the main and subheadings after you read the chapter. Do not neglect looking at the title and making connections between the title and the outline. Evaluate the appropriateness of the chapter title after you are finished reading the chapter. Remember that the key to successful studying is to INTERACT with the text as much as possible.

4. Vocabulary: To make vocabulary even more useful to you in studying, make sure you look at the entire sentence and understand the word in its context. Take the word "forte" below as an example. Do not just look up the word in the dictionary. How are the authors using the word? They are applying it here to Jay Gould who was an example of a ruthless speculator who was talented at, and notorious for, questionable financial maneuvers.

monopoly, p. 549	aesthetic, p. 562
consolidation, p. 551	gilded, p. 567
financiers, p. 554	cosmopolitan, p. 570
depressions, p. 557	philanthropists, p. 572
amenable, p. 559	cabarets, p. 573

5. Maps: Study Tip: When you look at the maps or develop your own, you should reinforce your knowledge by asking yourself the importance of each location or piece of information on the map. Why is this particular city, river, state, battle, or other location significant in this chapter? Following this practice is another way to interact with, reinforce and review material. An assortment of blank maps are attached to the end of this study guide. You can photocopy them to practice map skills.
   a. *Patterns of Industry, 1900: (p.* 552) Where was industrial manufacturing concentrated in 1900? What states were the major sources of materials such as iron ore and coal?
   b. *Population of Foreign Birth by Region, 1880:* (p. 561*)* Where did the majority of European immigrants settle in this period? Which area was affected the least? In what areas do you find French Canadians, Cubans and Mexicans in 1880?

RECITE/REVIEW

MULTIPLE CHOICE:

1. If you were a skilled worker in Packingtown, you were MOST likely to be
   a. Lithuanian.
   b. Scandanavian.
   c. German or Irish.
   d. Russian or Polish.

2. Which one of the following was NOT one of the elements that bound the Packingtown community to the national economic network?
   a. Chicago was a gateway city or destination point for raw materials and export of products.
   b. Chicago meat packer magnates exemplified monopoly capitalism.
   c. Huge factories had efficient production schedules.
   d. The most successful organized labor groups were there.

3. Thomas Alva Edison's laboratory in Menlo Park, New Jersey was one of the first to be devoted to
   a. improving worker efficiency.   c. solving environmental problems.
   b. industrial research.   d. fighting diseases.

4. While there were many new inventions, the basis of industrial growth in the decades after the Civil War was
   a. mining.   c. the railroad.
   b. meat-packing.   d. textile manufacturing.

5. During the economic boom of the mid-to-late 1800s, the geographic center of manufacturing kept moving
   a. north.   c. east.
   b. south.   d. west.

6. The United Fruit Company was to vertical integration as THIS company was to horizontal combination:
   a. U.S. Steel   c. Standard Oil
   b. Sears and Roebuck   d. American Tobacco

7. Vertical integration is to the control of production of a product as horizontal combination is to control of
   a. the market for a product.   c. the boards and financiers.
   b. the labor force.   d. all raw materials.

8. Ironically, the Sherman Anti-Trust Act was interpreted by the courts to inhibit growth of THIS GROUP rather than the industrial giants it was meant to control:
   a. city political machines   c. research labs
   b. trade unions   d. banks

9. Which one of the following would be LEAST likely to espouse the "gospel of wealth?"
   a. Russell Conwell   c. Andrew Carnegie
   b. George McNeil   d. Jay Gould

10. In 1883, a year of "minor" recession, this percentage of industrial workers in America lived below the poverty line:
    a. ten   c. forty
    b. twenty-five   d. fifty

11. Which one of the following unions had the LEAST in common with the other three?
    a. American Federation of Labor c. National Labor Union
    b. Eight Hour League   d. Knights of Labor

12. The violence in the Haymarket Square incident was an example of
    a. the turmoil in the urban ghettos.
    b. racial tensions between African Americans and new European immigrants.
    c. hostilities that broke out in large crowds at sporting events.
    d. hostility to labor union organizing.

13. By 1890 what fraction of Americans were city dwellers?
    a. one-fifth   c. one-third
    b. one-fourth   d. one-half

14. The new style of spending of the rich was labeled THIS by sociologist Thorstein Veblen:
    a. customs of incorporation   c. the Gilded Age
    b. conspicuous consumption   d. gospel of wealth

15. When the owners of fancy hotels and gambling houses realized that entertainment for the masses could pay, they opened a/an
    a. baseball stadium.   c. vaudeville theater.
    b. race track.   d. amusement park.

16. Which one of the following is NOT correctly matched to their accomplishment(s)?
    a. Louis Sullivan/skyscraper architect
    b. Booker T. Washington/Tuskegee founder and educator
    c. Henry W. Grady/New South editor
    d. John Roebling/baseball and sports entrepreneur

CHRONOLOGY AND MAP QUESTIONS:

17. Which one of the following events did not occur in 1882?
    a. Nineteenth century immigration to the United States peaks at 1.2 million.
    b. The Sherman Antitrust Act is passed.
    c. Congress passes the Chinese Exclusion Act.
    d. Standard Oil Trust is founded.

18. Severe depressions occurred in
    a. 1873 and 1893.   c. 1881 and 1891.
    b. 1870 and 1890.   d. 1866 and 1896.

19. In 1900 patterns of industry, you would find the MOST coal mining in these states:
    a. Washington, Oregon, Idaho, and Nevada
    b. Illinois, Ohio, Kentucky, Michigan, and Iowa
    c. Utah, Colorado, New Mexico and Arizona
    d. Alabama, Georgia, South and North Carolina

20. Very few of the immigrants in the 1880s went to this region of the United States:
    a. the South
    b. the Pacific Coast
    c. the Northeast
    d. the Southwest

SHORT ESSAY:

21. Who were the winners and the losers of the "Incorporation of America?"

22. The unionization movement harmed whom?

23. Why did immigrants tend to cluster with people of similar ethnic backgrounds?

24. What elements of American life brought different ethnic groups together?

EXTENDED ESSAY:

25. Describe how the "Gospel of Wealth" could be used as a justification for "Conspicuous Consumption."

26. Why does it seem reasonable that enthusiasm for sports and other forms of entertainment would have become so great during the "Gilded Age?"

27. Compare and contrast Rockefeller's and Carnegie's rise to commercial dominance in their respective fields.

ANSWERS-CHAPTER 19

MULTIPLE CHOICE:
1. c, p. 548	6. c, p. 553	11. a, p. 558-9
2. d, p. 549	7. a, p. 553	12. d, p. 558
3. b, p. 550	8. b, p. 554	13. c, p. 559
4. c, p. 550	9. b, p. 554-5	14. b, p. 667
5. d, p. 550	10. c, p. 557	15. d, p. 671
		16. d, p. 562

CHRONOLOGY AND MAP QUESTIONS:
17. b, p. 674	19. b, p. 552
18. a, p. 674	20. a, p. 561

SHORT ESSAY: 21-24

EXTENDED ESSAY: 25-27

COMMONWEALTH AND EMPIRE, 1870—1900

SURVEY

Chapter Overview: This chapter covers the conflicts between the populists and those groups that held the wealth and power. Mass political movements of farmers and workers were organized. These movements were also actively supported and shaped by women in addition to struggling for their own rights. There was a moment of democratic promise that was lost when Americans might have established a commonwealth based on agreement of the people for the common good. Instead a national governing class and a large bureaucratic state emerged. While debating their future, most Americans seemed united in pursuing an empire. Anti-imperialists lost as the U.S. acquired numerous territories and took an interventionist stance toward others.

Chapter Objectives: After reading the chapter and following the study suggestions given, you should be able to:

1. Explain the meaning of "a moment of democratic promise" as envisioned by Edward Bellamy and his followers in Point Loma, California as well as other reformers and populist organizers.
2. Describe the effects of the rapid expansion of government that paralleled the rapid growth of the economy in the late nineteenth century.
3. Describe the alternative governmental system as viewed by the Populist movement.
4. Discuss the crisis of the 1890s and the effects it had on people's view of the political system.
5. Explain why the election of 1896 was a turning point in American politics.
6. Summarize the interests and issues that persuaded many Americans of the need for an overseas empire.
7. Outline the steps by which the United States gained an empire and developed a foreign policy for that empire.
8. Summarize the arguments of the anti-imperialists.
9. Making Connections: Chapters Nineteen and Twenty: Compare the gospel of wealth to the social gospel.

QUESTIONS/READ

AMERICAN COMMUNITIES: **The Cooperative Commonwealth:** What was the nature of the community that some Americans like Edward Bellamy envisioned? Identify: Edward Bellamy's *Looking Backward* and his sequel novel, *Equality,* industrial army, "new nation," Point Loma, California, Katjerome Tingley, "a moment of democratic promise."

TOWARD A NATIONAL GOVERNING CLASS: What was the national governing class that emerged? How did it consolidate in the modern two-party system as well as in the federal governmental bureaucracy? What reforms were enacted?

> **The Growth of the Government:** How and why did governmental services develop and grow at all levels? What other federal bodies were founded or expanded at this time? What was the Interstate Commerce Commission and what was its significance in terms of governmental power? What was the result for the federal government's power?
>
> **The Machinery of Politics:** How did the growth of government affect the machinery of politics? What type of record or principles did each party present? What type of consistency was there to each party's principles? How did the power of the president compare to Congress or to the state legislatures? What were the voting patterns of the parties and the branches of government they controlled? What type of voter participation was there? How did parties pay for the cost of organizations and campaigns? What was John Jay Chapman's observation? Identify: boodle, spoils.
>
> **One Politician's Story:** How was James Garfield a typical politician of this age? How did ordinary citizens see government? What was Bellamy's recommendation?
>
> **The Spoils System and Civil Service Reform:** What was the spoils system and how extensive was it? What reform was proposed and enacted? What was the Pendleton Act and what effect did it have on patronage? What was the position of lawyers in national politics? Identify: Circuit Court of Appeals Act of 1891.

FARMERS AND WORKERS ORGANIZE THEIR COMMUNITIES: What type of political movement did many farmers and workers develop? What were the principles of this Populist movement?

> **The Grange:** What was the Grange and what were its principles? How did it become a political organization? What were the major grievances of farmers? Who did they see as their enemies and what types of reforms did they want? What happened to the Grange by 1880 and what longer lasting effects did it have? Identify: Oliver H. Kelley, thieves in the night, *Munn v. Illinois.*
>
> **The Farmer's Alliance:** What types of farmer organizations developed after the Grange and where were they located? What were their principles? How did they operate differently from the Grange and what successes did they have? Identify: Charles W. Macune, National Farmers' Alliance and Industrial Union, national Colored Farmers' Alliance and Cooperative Union, Southern and Northern Farmers' Alliance.
>
> **Workers Search for Power:** What types of organizations did the workers develop? What were the Tompkins Square Riot and the "Great Uprising of 1877"? How did authorities react to each and what other general effects were there? What happened to most of the labor groups and what long range effects did they have? Who was Henry George and what

was he symbolic of? Identify: Law and Order League, National Guard, Progress and Poverty.

Women Build Alliances: What type of alliances were built within men's organizations as well as specific women's groups? Who was Frances E. Willard and what beliefs and views did she have? What was the extent of influence of the WCTU? How did the Populist movement react to women as members? Identify: Leonora M. Barry, Mary E. Lease, *Farmer's Wife,* Annie Diggs.

Farmer-Labor Unity: How did farmer-labor unity develop and what influence did it have in American politics? How well did they fare in the 1892 election? Identify: People's Party Platform, Ignatius Donnelly, "pepper and salt."

THE CRISIS OF THE 1890s: What were the events that made up the crisis of the 1890s? How did government and the political parties respond? What conflicts resulted? Identify: Ignatius Donnelly, *Caesar's Column.*

Financial Collapse and the Depression: What caused the financial collapse and resulting depression? What was the extent of the depression? What types of problems arose and what were the responses from government? Identify: Philadelphia and Reading Railroad, vagrancy laws, Jacob Sechler Coxey.

Strikes and the Solidarity of Labor: How united was the labor movement during the 1890s? What were the circumstances and outcome of the Homestead strike against the Carnegie Steel Company? In what way had the union defeated itself? What were the circumstances and outcome of the Pullman strike and how did Eugene V. Debs try to avoid the mistakes at Homestead? What did Debs go on to do in the late 1800s and early 1900s? Identify: Amalgamated Iron, Steel and Tin Workers, Henry C. Frick, George Pullman, Eugene V. Debs, American Railway Union.

The Social Gospel: Who were the main leaders of the social gospel movement and what did they call for? What groups did the social gospel appeal to? Identify: *Applied Christianity,* Beulahland, *If Christ Came to Chicago, If Jesus Came to Boston, In His Steps, Rerum Novarum,* Young Women's Christian Association.

POLITICS OF REFORM, POLITICS OF ORDER: What was the conflict between the advocates of reform and those who valued order? How did the political parties line up on these issues? What was the outcome?

The Free-Silver Issue: What was the free silver issue? What positions were taken by the political parties? What groups favored and what groups opposed the free coinage of silver? What was President Cleveland's response? Identify: "soft" currency, greenbacks, 1873 Coinage Act, Sherman Silver Purchase Act, McKinley Tariff, Silver Democrats, William McKinley.

Populism's Last Campaigns: What was the problem for Populists in the 1896 election? Who was William Jennings Bryan and how did he fit in the free silver controversy and Populist ranks? Identify: David Waite, "Cross of Gold" speech, Democratic-Populist ticket.

The Limits of Democracy: What were the limits of democracy in terms of both presidential candidates? What types of actions eroded the rights of African Americans? What various rulings of the Supreme Court further limited African American rights? What view did the era's major reformers and protest movements have on racial and ethnic prejudice? Who was Ida B. Wells and what did her investigation show? What successes did she have? Identify: American Protective Association, Jim Crow laws, civil rights cases, *Plessy v. Ferguson, Cumming v. Richmond County Board of Education,* grandfather clauses, *Red Record,* National Association of Colored Women.

Tom Watson: Who was Tom Watson and what does his story illustrate? What views and programs did Tom Watson advocate and how popular was he? What happened to him later?

THE IMPERIALISM OF RIGHTEOUSNESS: What was the "imperialism of righteousness" and what economic motivations were behind it? How was imperialism propelled both by Christian missionaries and economic and political ones? Identify: Albert J. Beveridge.

The White Man's Burden: What was the notion of the white man's burden? How did Frederick Jackson Turner's ideas fit into imperialism? How was the World's Fair in Chicago symbolic of imperialist issues and American notions of superiority? What were the views of Frederick Douglass and Ida B. Wells on the World's Fair? Who was Josiah Strong and what were his views of empire? What were the views of Beveridge?

Foreign Missions: How did foreign missions coincide with imperialism? What groups did the mission field appeal to? What successes did they have? What was meant by America's three occupying forces: army, navy, and the "Y"? What overseas area was the most popular with missionaries and merchants alike? How did Josiah Strong express the connection of economics and religion?

An Overseas Empire: What areas did the United States acquire as empire? Who was William H. Seward and what was his role in empire building ideas? What areas did he actually acquire? How did the United States advocates of empire view the nations south and north of the United States? What actually happened? Who was Alfred Thayer Mahan and what argument did he present in *The Influence of Sea Power upon History, 1660-1873*? How did the U.S. annex Hawaii and what was the economic connection? How was Hawaii viewed in relation to the Pacific? What were the views of Secretaries of State James Blaine and John Hay? Identify: American lake, Good Neighbor Policy, Pan-American Conference, Great White Fleet, Naval War College, Liliuokalani, ocean bride, Open Door, Boxer Rebellion.

THE SPANISH-AMERICAN WAR: What were the causes and results of the Spanish-American War? What were the views of President McKinley on the war?

A "Splendid Little War" in Cuba: Who viewed the war as a "splendid little war?" Why did Americans want Cuba? How did Presidents Cleveland and McKinley react to the growing conflict? What events brought America into the war? What was the Senate vote on the war resolution? How was Cuba dealt with after the war? Identify: José Marti, *Maine,* Teller Amendment, Rough Riders, Platt Amendment, Cuban-American Treaty of 1903, Puerto Rico, Virgin Islands, Guam.

War in the Philippines: How did the U.S. gain the Philippines? What was the policy of President McKinley? Why did the Filipino rebels turn against the U.S.? Why was the American action referred to as a modern guerrilla war? What was the outcome? What were the ideas expressed in Strong's *Expansion?* Identify: Theodore Roosevelt, George Dewey, Emilio Aquinaldo, *"gu-gus."*

Critics of Empire: What individuals and groups made up the critics of empire? What were the contrary arguments of the anti-imperialists? What was the Anti-Imperialist League and what actions did they take? How did the two broad lines of dissent show themselves in the League? What views did the press have of the war? What was the public attitude?

CONCLUSION: What was the end result for populists who wanted to retain community self-government? What happened instead?

CHRONOLOGY: Apply the standard questions from Chapter 17, p.11 of the Study Guide.

STUDY SKILLS EXERCISES

1. Making connections: Be alert to making connections between chapters. The authors of your text always have a sentence in their conclusion section that ties into the next chapter. In addition, you are given objectives and sample essay questions in this review guide that point out connections. Make this work for you when studying. Your professor may have essay questions on the test that require you to synthesize information across chapters. You must be alert yourself to connections since not all of the possibilities could be included in the study guide. Notice that Chapters eighteen, nineteen, and twenty all cover the same time period. Some common themes are the economic growth of America as well as arguments about what was best for America. Would all Americans be included? An example of a question your instructor might ask: Discuss the extent to which all Americans were included in the economic boom and growth from 1860 to 1900. Include a consideration of groups excluded and what steps they tried to take to change things. How well was America fulfilling its democratic promise? If your course starts with Chapter Seventeen on Reconstruction, be sure to include this in your connection making.

2. Make a chart on the money question. It should be a two-column chart with the gold standard or hard money issue in one column and the silver standard or soft money in the other. Your topics to consider for each issue could be items such as the basis of each system, the advantages and disadvantages, political issues related to them, groups in favor and groups against, significant election results laws that were passed, and outcome of the issue by 1900. You will find a sample blank at the end of this chapter.

3. Reflections:
   a. Imagine a debate between imperialists and anti-imperialists. What points would each side make? For further ideas, take specific individual parts as Josiah Strong, Ida Wells, Emilio Equinaldo, Samuel Gompers.
   b. It is not quite the year 2000 but imagine how Edward Bellamy would react if he "reappeared" here in the late-1990s. What do you think he would say? How would Ignatius Donnelly react?

4. In the vocabulary below is the word *commonwealth*. Remember, if you are not sure what these words mean, look them up. One meaning of the word commonwealth is a republic or

a state founded and united by compact or agreement of the people for the common good or the commonwealth, the general welfare. How did this sense of community clash with imperialism as America expanded at home and overseas? Who was included and who was left out of the commonwealth? Include any relevant information from previous chapters Seventeen to Nineteen.

5. Vocabulary:

utopia, p. 579	socialist, p. 592
partisans, p. 583	specie, p. 593
suffrage, p. 584	egalitarian, p. 597
usurious, p. 586	annexation, p. 601
solidarity, p. 589	guerilla, p. 604

6. Maps:
    a. *Strikes by State, 1880:* (p. 587) What three states had the greatest number of strikes after the uprising of 1877? Which five states had the second highest rate? Where were most of these strikes concentrated? What general areas had the least number of strikes?
    b. *Election of 1896, by States:* (p. 595) What areas of the country did each candidate carry? What types of areas were they? Notice that the popular vote was not that far apart for both candidates but the electoral vote was. Why was that?
    c. *The American Domain:* (p. 600) In what two general areas was the United States involved? Be able to locate: Cuba, Puerto Rico, Alaska, Hawaii, Guam, Midway, the Philippines.
    d. *The Spanish-American War:* (p. 602) What were the two theaters of action in the war? The war was largely a naval operation, what two water bodies were involved? Be able to locate: Manila, Santiago.

RECITE/REVIEW

MULTIPLE CHOICE:

1. Which one of the following was NOT one of Edward Bellamy's concepts in his novel, *Looking Backward?*
    a. Automated machinery will eliminate most menial tasks.
    b. The United States would be a cooperative commonwealth.
    c. Communities collectively own businesses.

2. The Point Loma community actually tried to create Bellamy's community ideas and
    a. managed to survive into the 1950s.
    b. failed within the first year.
    c. were not able to fulfill their children's education.
    d. were destroyed by rioters who considered them anarchists.

3. Bellamy hoped citizens would mobilize nationwide and
   a. establish cooperative communities throughout the world.
   b. overturn the existing political and economic leadership.
   c. work against the building of empire.
   d. create an international union.

4. Which one of the following was NOT a federal agency or department that grew or began during this period from 1870 to 1900?
   a. Treasury   c. Labor
   b. Veterans Bureau   d. Defense

5. From 1877 to 1893 the position of president of the United States was basically
   a. a weak position yielding to Congress and state legislatures.
   b. a powerful position directing Congress and the Courts.
   c. powerful in foreign policy but weak in domestic affairs.
   d. well established as a position of representing the "forgotten American."

6. The Pendleton Reform Act attempted to reform what area?
   a. civil rights   c. civil service
   b. railroad rates   d. public education

7. Which one of the following groups would be the LEAST likely to have many populists in it?
   a. farmers   c. workers
   b. business executives   d. African Americans

8. Which one of these would NOT be in a Granger's list of "thieves in the night."
   a. railroads
   b. farm equipment manufacturers
   c. banks
   d. labor unions

9. The Tompkins Square Riot and the Great Uprising of 1877 were both examples of reactions by
   a. white laborers against African Americans and foreigners.
   b. laborers demanding rights during the economic panic.
   c. National Guard soldiers against urban rioters.
   d. nationwide farmer alliances against big business and big government.

10. If you were a member of the largest organization of women in the world in the late nineteenth century, you would belong to the
    a. Women's Christian Temperance Union.
    b. Women's Union Missionary Society of Americans for Heathen Lands.
    c. National American Woman Suffrage Association.
    d. Young Women's Christian Association.

11. The People's Party or Populists ran the strongest in the 1892 election in this area of the country:
    a. New England
    b. Upper South
    c. Great Plains and the West
    d. Midwest

12. The financial collapse and depression of the 1890s was precipitated by the downfall of this company in March 1893:
    a. U.S. Steel
    b. Standard Oil Refineries
    c. Union Pacific Railroad
    d. Philadelphia and Reading Railroad

13. In 1894 Jacob Coxey gathered an army. The members were
    a. part of Bellamy's concept of an industrial army.
    b. demanding a public works program to create jobs.
    c. women who were going to storm saloons to enforce prohibition.
    d. amalgamated strikers who were planning to storm Carnegie Steel.

14. If you were in favor of soft currency in the 1890s, you would be LEAST likely to support
    a. the gold standard.
    b. treasury notes.
    c. free coinage of silver.
    d. inflated currency.

15. If you believed in the promise of "a full dinner pail" in the 1900 election, then you voted for
    a. William Jennings Bryan.
    b. Tom Watson.
    c. William McKinley.
    d. Grover Cleveland.

16. Which one of the following authors is NOT correctly matched to their book?
    a. Washington Gladden/*Applied Christianity*
    b. F. J. Turner/*The Significance of the Frontier in American History*
    c. Josiah Strong/*Expansion*
    d. George Dewey/*The Influence of Sea Power upon History*

17. Which one of the following is NOT an area of empire gained by the United States up to and including the McKinley administration?
    a. Panama Canal
    b. Philippines
    c. Hawaii
    d. Puerto Rico

18. Both the Teller and Platt Amendments illustrate the conflict of Americans over
    a. recognizing unions.
    b. allowing any foreign trade and overseas investment.
    c. acquiring empire, in this case Cuba.
    d. various populist issues.

CHRONOLOGY AND MAP QUESTIONS:

19. Which one of the following is the CORRECT order for these events?
    (1) McKinley re-elected   (3) Pendleton Civil Service Reform
    (2) Hawaii annexed   (4) Alaska purchased
    a. 4,3,2,1   c. 4,2,3,1
    b. 2,4,1,3   d. 1,2,4,3

20. Which one of the following is the CORRECT order for these labor events?
    (1) Coxey's Army marches   (3) Tompkins Square Riot
    (2) Great Uprising of 1877   (4) Homestead steelworkers strike
    a. 2,1,4,3   c. 4,1,3,2
    b. 1,4,2,3   d. 3,2,4, 1

21. *Plessy v. Ferguson* establishes segregation as "separate but equal" in
    a. 1876.   c. 1896.
    b. 1888.   d. 1899.

22. Which one of the following states is NOT one of those with the highest strike rates in 1880?
    a. Ohio   c. New York
    b. Florida   d. Pennsylvania

23. William Jennings Bryan won the most support in these states in the 1896 election:
    a. New England   c. the West and South
    b. the Midwest   d. the Northeast

SHORT ESSAY:

24. Why did citizens in the North and South hold differing views on the use of tariffs?

25. Describe Bryan's "Free Silver" campaign.

26. What was the "White Man's Burden?"

EXTENDED ESSAY:

27. Why was organized labor nativistic?

28. In what ways did economic concerns drive American imperialism?

29. In what ways did religious fervor drive American imperialism?

30. In what ways did American expansion run counter to the country's founding ideals?

ANSWERS-CHAPTER 20

MULTIPLE CHOICE:
1. d, p. 579	6. c, p. 584	11. c, p. 589	16. d, p. 600
2. a, p. 580	7. b, p. 585-7	12. d, p. 590	17. a, p. 600-5
3. b, p. 579	8. d, p. 585	13. b, p. 590	18. c, p. 603
4. d, p. 581-2	9. b, p. 587	14. a, p. 593	
5. a, p. 583	10. a, p. 588	15. c, p. 595	

CHRONOLOGY AND MAP QUESTIONS:
19. a, p. 605	21. c, p. 605	23. c, p. 595
20. d, p. 605	22. b, p. 587	

SHORT ESSAY:
24-26

EXTENDED ESSAY:
27-30

Basis of the System	Gold Standard of Hard Money	Silver Standard or Soft Money
Advantages		
Dis-advantages		
Related Political Issues		
Groups in Favor		
Groups Against		
Significant Election Results		
Laws Passed		
Outcome of Issue By 1900		

URBAN AMERICA AND THE PROGRESSIVE ERA, 1900—1917

SURVEY

Chapter Overview: This chapter covers continued urbanization of America and the social problems that resulted from rapid unplanned growth of the cities. Both political bosses and reformers tried to respond to the reality of industrialized and urbanized America. Social Darwinism was challenged by the Progressives who had a new, sometimes inconsistent, vision of the American community. They viewed the government as an ally to achieve realistic and pragmatic reforms. The climate for reform came from social workers, social scientists at universities and investigative journalists. Both political parties would embrace progressive views. Presidents Roosevelt, Taft and Wilson based their programs on these new ideas. Although much was accomplished, the progressive movement lacked unity and failed to address issues of class, race or sex adequately. Legislation was not always enforced or had unintended negative consequences. In the long run, politics was affected by the demand for social justice and attempts were made to confront the problems of rapid industrialization and urbanization.

Chapter Objectives: After reading the chapter and following the study suggestions given, you should be able to:

1. Trace the process by which the women settlement house workers first began and the community of reform they tried to create.
2. Summarize the principles of the progressives, and the views of its principal proponents in journalism, social sciences and government, as well as its legacy.
3. Discuss the aims of and problems with social control legislation desired by the progressives.
4. Outline the problems of working class communities and their attempts to solve them through unions and reform legislation.
5. Summarize the role of women in the reform campaigns and the effects it had on their participation in public life and leadership positions.
6. Summarize the difficulties of black progressives in gaining recognition but also positive effects within the black community.
7. Outline the attempts by both the Democratic and Republican parties to respond to demands that the governments, local, state and national, address the issues of social justice.

8. Making connections: chapters nineteen to twenty-one: analyze the possible connections between populism and progressivism as social reform movements.

QUESTIONS/READ

AMERICAN COMMUNITIES: **The Henry Street Settlement House: Women Settlement House Workers Create A Community of Reform:** What was the Henry Street Settlement House and how did it become a model reform community? What issues did settlement houses try to address? What group generally lived in and worked for settlement houses? How rapidly did the settlement idea grow from 1891 to 1910? What did the Henry Street House accomplish? Identify: Lillian Wald, Jane Addams, National Association for the Advancement of Colored People, "The whole world is my neighborhood."

THE CURRENTS OF PROGRESSIVISM: What problems originally inspired progressivism at the state level? What is the problem with defining progressivism?

Unifying Themes: What were the themes of progressivism at the state and national level? What were the sources of inspiration for the progressive movement? What uneasy combination did progressivism offer?

Women Spearhead Reform: Why did settlement house workers go beyond private charity to confront the social and political systems? Who was Jane Addams and what did she add to social progressivism? Who was Florence Kelley and what were her accomplishments and writings? What was their legacy? Identify: Hull House, subjective necessity, *Hull House Maps and Papers,* Lillian Wald.

The Urban Machine: What services did the urban political machines offer and how did they respond to the progressives? What were the views of George W. Plunkitt and Timothy Sullivan? How powerful was machine politics? What machine politicians ally themselves with progressives and on what types of reforms?

Political Progressives and Urban Reform: What was the connection between political progressives and urban reforms? What types of problems did big cities face? Why did progressives concentrate on the structure of government and what changes did they propose? What were the commission and city manager forms of government? Who were Samuel Jones and Thomas L. Johnson and what type of approach did they follow? Identify: National Municipal League.

Progressivism in the Statehouse: How did progressivism fare at the state level? What states and individual leaders were significant and what types of reforms did they enact? What was their record on racism and "Jim Crow" laws? Identify: Wisconsin Idea, initiative, referendum, direct primary, recall.

New Journalism: Muckraking: What was new about journalism and what was the muckraking element in it? Who were the significant muckrakers and what were their writings? What problems did they draw attention to and what effect did they have? Identify: Jacob Riis, S.S. McClure, Lincoln Steffens, Ida Tarbell, Ray Stannard Baker, exposure journalism, Meat Inspection Act, Pure Food and Drug Act.

Intellectual Currents Promoting Reform: What new intellectual ideas helped support progressivism? What challenge did sociologists like Lester Frank Ward offer to social Darwinism? What were John Dewey's views on education? How did some of the social scientists contribute directly to reform? What were the basic ideas of John Commons and Richard Ely? What happened to the use of the Fourteenth Amendment? What was the significance of legal dissenters like Oliver Wendel Holmes and Louis Brandeis? Identify: social sciences, telic, genetic, *Gemeinschaft, Gesellschaft, ethical elite*, embyronic communities, *Lochner v. New York*, sociological jurisprudence, *Muller v. Oregon*, Brandeis Brief, Edward Ross.

SOCIAL CONTROL AND ITS LIMITS: How was social control part of the progressive view? At which groups was this social control aimed? How successful was it? Identify: Eugenics.

The Prohibition Movement: What was the focus of the various temperance groups like the WCTU and the Anti-Saloon League? What groups were likely to support prohibition and what groups were likely to oppose it? What was the pietist vs. ritualist issue? Overall how successful was the movement at the state and then federal level?

The Social Evil: What was the social evil? Why was there more intensity about prostitution at this point? What were the various issues relative to prostitution? How did the progressive bent for studying problems via statistics show itself in this era? What did they find? What reforms did they enact and what unintended effects did they have? Identify: Charles K. Parkhurst, white slave, Mann Act.

The Redemption of Leisure: How did the progressives see leisure as a moral issue? What leisure activities were particularly threatening? How was this particularly expressed by Frederick C. Howe? Identify: nickelodeon, movie palace? National Board of Censorship.

Standardizing Education: What goals did progressives set for educating children? How was one of the goals expressed by Elwood Cubberley? How rapidly did education grow from 1890 to 1918? What were the main principles of education as expressed in the National Education Association report of 1918? Identify; Smith-Hughes Act of 1917, College Entrance Examination Board, E.L. Thorndike.

WORKING-CLASS COMMUNITIES AND PROTEST: What types of workingclass communities were there and what issues were they concerned with? What were the numbers of farm workers versus industrial workers? How successful were their protests?

The New Immigrants: What proportion of industrial labor was foreign-born? Where were most of them from? How were they different than earlier immigrants? What did many newcomers plan to do? What did the statistics of the U.S. Steel Mill in 1907 tell us about immigrant labor? What other groups immigrated to the U.S. and where and in what businesses did they concentrate? Identify: chains, Issei, Nisei, barrios.

Urban Ghettos: What was the immigrant experience in the urban ghettos? How was New York City an example of this? How did progressive reformers enter the union picture? What was the uprising of the 20,000 and what power did it illustrate? What was the Triangle Shirtwaist Company issue and the result? Identify: piece-rate system, Women's Trade Union League, ILGWU, Clara Lemlich, Pauline Newman, Rose Schneiderman.

Company Towns: What were the advantages and disadvantages of living in a company town? How did the community try to mediate with the company? What did a 1910 study of work accidents reveal? What was scientific management and the counter-action of "slowing down" or "soldiering?" What did Ludlow and Trinidad show about company towns and their power? What was the Ludlow Massacre and what results did it have?

The AFL: Unions, Pure and Simple: Why was the AFL termed a "union, pure and simple?" How successful was Gompers and the AFL? What weakness was there to their exclusive policy? Identify: United Mine Workers, National Association of Manufacturers, "open shop," *Loewe v. Lawler,* secondary boycott.

The IWW: One Big Union: What was the "one big union" concept of the IWW? Where was the IWW most popular and why? Who was William Haywood and why did he denounce the AFL? What was their overall success? Identify: "Bread and Roses" strike, McNamara Brothers.

Rebels In Bohemia: Who were the rebels and where was "Bohemia?" What was the meaning of the term Bohemian and what were they symbolic of? What sense of community were they seeking?

WOMEN'S MOVEMENTS AND BLACK AWAKENING: How did the progressive ideology affect women's groups and African American groups?

The New Woman: How did the progressive movement provide new avenues for women? What women were particularly attracted to the movement and why? How many women had a higher education? Why were these clubs likely to turn to reforms and what types of reform did they concentrate on? How did it encourage a sense of community among women? Identify: General Federation of Women's Clubs, National Consumers League, white label, Florence Kelley, social housekeeping.

Birth Control: How did the birth control movement begin and who organized and led it? How successful was Margaret Sanger and what organizations did she found?

Racism and Accommodation: How widespread was racism and violence against African Americans from the 1890s through the early 1900s? What was Booker T. Washington's idea of accommodation? What did he encourage blacks to focus on? Why did he gain white support? Identify: Thomas Dixon's *The Clansman,* Tuskegee Institute, *Up From Slavery,* National Negro Business League.

Racial Justice and the NAACP: What alternative to Washington's accommodation became more popular? Who was W.E.B. DuBois and what alternative leadership did he give? Identify: A *Red Record,* National Association of Colored Women, *The Souls of Black Folk,* "double consciousness, "talented tenth," Niagara Movement, NAACP, *The Crisis.*

NATIONAL PROGRESSIVISM: What form did progressivism take at the national level? What presidents embraced the ideas and how did it affect the office of the president? What groups would rival the political parties?

Theodore Roosevelt and Presidential Activism: How did Roosevelt view the office of president and how did he proceed to make the most of his view? How did Roosevelt's style encourage progressivism? How did he view his responsibility and how did he think problems could be solved? Identify: bully pulpit.

Trust-Busting and Regulation: What trust-busting and business regulation did Roosevelt undertake? How successful was he? What was he trying to assert and what was his view about breaking up all large corporations? What three measures did he get passed in Congress and what was the basic belief behind all three of them? Why did some large businesses support regulation? Identify: *Northern Securities v. U.S.,* trust-buster.

Conservation, Preservation, and the Environment: What position did Roosevelt take on preservation versus conservation? What view did Pinchot take? Who was John Muir and what view did he represent? What actions had Muir taken to try and publicize his view as well as save specific areas? How did the Hetch Hetchy Valley issue illustrate the differences between Muir and Pinchot? What was the outcome? Identify: U.S. Forest Service, Gifford Pinchot, Yosemite Act of 1890, Sierra Club, National Park Service, Newlands Reclamation Act.

Republican Split: Why did Roosevelt's view of reform split the Republican Party? What happened to the split when Taft took office? How did Taft compare to Roosevelt? Why did Roosevelt return to politics and form the Progressive Party? What was his "New Nationalism" program? Identify: Square Deal.

The Election of 1912: Who were the candidates and what were the issues in the election of 1912? On what basis did Wilson claim the Democratic Party to be the true progressives? What was his "New Freedom" program? What effect did Socialist candidate Eugene V. Debs have on the campaigns of Wilson and Roosevelt? What was the outcome of the election? How well did the Socialists do? Why was this the first "modern" presidential race?

Woodrow Wilson's First Term: What did Wilson do in his first term and what program did his actions resemble? What social issues did Wilson champion and what were his limitations? Identify: Underwood Simmons Act, Sixteenth Amendment, Federal Reserve Act, Clayton Anti-Trust Act, Federal Trade Commission.

CONCLUSION: What was the progressive legacy? Where did it fall short?

CHRONOLOGY: Apply the standard questions from p. 4 of the Study Guide.

STUDY SKILLS EXERCISES:

1. Reflection: There are a number of debates that you could reflect on and as you do, consider your own views on the subject .
   a. Imagine a debate between Booker T. Washington and W.E.B. DuBois. What issues would be discussed? What points would be made?
   b. Imagine a debate between Gifford Pinchot and John Muir. What issues would be discussed? What points would be made?
2. Making connections:
   a. Modern day political candidates, both Republican and Democrat and third parties as well, like to invoke Theodore Roosevelt's name and somehow try to claim his legacy. Why do you think they pick Roosevelt so often?
   b. What was the connection between the social gospel and the progressive viewpoint?
   c. To what extent do we still debate many of the points of the Social Darwinists and Gospel of Wealth ideas versus the progressives and the Social Gospel?
3. A chart that might be helpful in this chapter would be to list the major writers, activists, and intellectuals down one side of the chart. Across the top list major ideas, writings, positions held, actions or organizations founded. A blank chart is attached to the end of this chapter.

4. Vocabulary:

rhetoric, p. 612	boycotts, p. 627
constituents, p. 615	anarchist, p. 629
dissident, p. 616	bohemian, p. 630
abysmal, p. 618	milieu, p. 630
parochial, p. 622	consecrate, p. 637

5. Maps:
   a. *Immigration, 1900-1920:* (p. 623) Where did most immigrants to the United States come from in the years between 1900 and 1920? How did this compare to the nineteenth century? What percent of the American labor force was made up of foreign-born? Match the map to the chart. What specific European countries ranked in the top four?

   b. *The Election of 1912:* (p. 637) What was significant about Woodrow Wilson's election as a Democrat? What happened in the Republican Party that worked to Wilson's advantage? How did Teddy Roosevelt's popular and electoral vote compare to Taft's? How did Debs fare as a candidate? Look at the 1896 election map on page 595. What states that voted for Wilson might have voted for Taft (or for Roosevelt if he had been the Republican candidate)? What areas did Wilson carry that Bryan failed to in 1896?

RECITE/REVIEW

MULTIPLE CHOICE:

1. Which one of the following is NOT true of settlement houses?
   a. They were reform communities run by college-educated women.
   b. They were in the midst of the neighborhoods they were trying to help.
   c. They grew from six in 1891 to 400 houses nationwide by 1910.
   d. They were progressives but were often anti-immigrant.

2. Which one of the following was NOT an activity of Lillian Wald's Henry House?
   a. providing health care for immigrants
   b. campaigning for school lunches
   c. working for conservation
   d. encouraging theater, music and dance

3. Lillian Wald was to Henry House as THIS person was to Hull House:
   a. Marv Brewster.   c. Florence Kelley.
   b. Jane Addams.   d. Rose Schneiderman.

4. Samuel "Golden Rule" Jones and Thomas L. Johnson were examples of city leader-reformers who advocated a change in
   a. policy to improve social welfare for city residents.
   b. the slums and ghetto buildings.
   c. government such as the city commission and manager systems.
   d. voting such as recall and referendum.

5. The "Wisconsin Idea" was promoted by Governor Bob LaFollette as a way of
   a. strengthening direct democracy with direct primaries and other political reforms.
   b. controlling large industries.
   c. protecting state forests and watersheds.
   d. applying academic scholarship and theory to the needs of people.

6. In Jacob Riis's book, *How the Other Half Lives,* the "other half" referred to the lives of
   a. women.
   b. African Americans.
   c. the urban poor.
   d. industrial magnates.

7. *McClure's* was a magazine that published exposés of the nation's social problems. One such series was Lincoln Steffen's study of widespread graft called *The Shame of the*
   a. *Railroads.*
   b. *Cities.*
   c. *Senate.*
   d. *Oil Companies.*

8. Not only was it a bestseller, but Upton Sinclair's muckraking novel, *The Jungle,* also resulted in these two federal laws:
   a. Clayton Anti-Trust Act and the Federal Trade Commission
   b. Mann Act and the National Board of Censorship
   c. National Municipal Act and Initiative, Referendum, and Recall Act
   d. Meat Inspection Act and the Pure Food and Drug Act

9. Theodore Roosevelt gave them the label "muckrakers." They were
   a. writers who exposed details of social and political evils.
   b. the corrupt political bosses in big city machines.
   c. pessimists who did not accept the progressive idea of reform.
   d. women who wanted more radical things than suffrage reform.

10. The state was to economist Richard Ely as THIS was to philosopher John Dewey:
    a. telic evolution
    b. education
    c. ethical shift
    d. *Gesellschaft*

11. You were MOST likely to be for prohibition if you were
    a. a working class Catholic.
    b. a German Lutheran.
    c. an urban Jew.
    d. a middle class Protestant.

12. If you were a teacher trying to follow Elwood Cubberley's ideas, you would be stressing
    a. vocational manual training programs for a new industrial order.
    b. educational psychology and guidance counseling.
    c. assimilation and "Americanization" of immigrant children.
    d. family education centers to help reform the slums.

13. The International Ladies Garment Workers Union gained strength and merged working class women with middle class reformers as a result of the
    a. Ludlow Massacre.   c. "Bread and Roses" strike.
    b. Triangle Shirtwaist Fire.   d. "Uprising of the 20,000."

14. In terms of racism, southern progressive reformers
    a. advocated complete equality.
    b. thought blacks were incapable of improvement.
    c. were less hostile but still paternalistic.
    d. felt blacks were not part of the New South.

15. Which one of the following has the LEAST association with the other three?
    a. double consciousness   c. talented tenth
    b. Niagara movement   d. *Up From Slavery*

16. Conservation was to the U.S. Forest Service as THIS was to the National Park Service:
    a. preservation   c. managed use
    b. business first   d. recreation

17. Which one of the following is NOT a reason that the election of 1912 was the first modern presidential race?
    a. It had the first direct primaries.
    b. There was a great deal of interest group activity.
    c. The candidates avoided issues and "threw mud" instead.
    d. Traditional party loyalties were challenged.

CHRONOLOGY AND MAP QUESTIONS:

18. Which one of the following describes the CORRECT order of these events?
    (1) Margaret Sanger begins writing and speaking on birth control.
    (2) Lillian Wald establishes Henry Street Settlement in New York.
    (3) Jane Addams founds Hull House in Chicago.
    (4) Florence Kelley leads National Consumers' League.
    a. 3,2,4,1   c. 2.3,4,1
    b. 4,2,3,1   d. 1,4,3,2

19. The National Association for the Advancement of Colored People (NAACP) was founded in
    a. 1889.   c. 1906.
    b. 1901.   d. 1909.

20. Woodrow Wilson takes the presidency in THIS year, defeating Taft, Roosevelt and Debs:
    a. 1900
    b. 1904
    c. 1908
    d. 1912

21. The Sixteenth Amendment is ratified in THIS year bringing in a graduated tax:
    a. 1889
    b. 1908
    c. 1913
    d. 1916

22. Which one of the following was NOT one of the top four European countries that was a source of immigrants to the United States between 1900 and 1920?
    a. Germany
    b. Austria-Hungary
    c. Poland
    d. Russia

23. Wilson was only the second Democrat since the Civil War to be elected to the presidency in 1912. He was able to do this because
    a. Eugene Debs drew votes away from the Republicans.
    b. he repeated McKinley's pattern in 1896.
    c. the Republicans split between Taft and Roosevelt.
    d. the state Democratic machines had revived.

SHORT ESSAY:

24. In what ways did the Progressive movement draw upon science for guidance?

25. How was education used to achieve Progressive goals?

26. Why was the Republican Party at such a disadvantage in the presidential election of 1912?

EXTENDED ESSAY:

27. In what ways did Wilson's background make him a natural Progressive Era presidential candidate?

28. Why did some big business figures support federal intrusion into the economy?

29. Why was birth control an important element in the liberation of women?

ANSWERS-CHAPTER 21

MULTIPLE CHOICE:
1. d, p. 610-11
2. c, p. 610-11
3. b, p. 614
4. a, p. 616
5. d, p. 617
6. c, p. 618
7. c, p. 618
8. d, p. 618
9. a, p. 618
10. b, p. 619
11. d, p. 620
12. c, p. 622
13. b, p. 626
14. c, p. 631
15. d, p. 632
16. a, p. 634-5
17. c, p. 637

CHRONOLOGY AND MAP:
18. a, p. 639
19. d, p. 639
20. d, p. 639
21. c, p. 639
22. a, p. 623
23. c, p. 637

SHORT ESSAY:
24-29

EXTENDED ESSAY:
27-29

CHAPTER 21: STUDY SKILLS EXERCISE #3

Name:	Position or Title(s)	Major Ideas/Programs	Actions (Writ/Legis/etc.)
Lilian Wald			
Jane Addams			
Florence Kelley			
Robert M. LaFollette			
Clara Lemlich			
William Haywood			
Jacob Riis			
Lincoln Steffens			
Ida Tarbell			
Ray Stannard Baker			
Upton Sinclair			
David Graham Phillips			
Lester Ward			
Edward Ross			
John Dewey			
John R. Commons			
Richard Ely			
Oliver Wendell Holmes			
Elwood Cubberly			
E.D. Thorndike			
Margaret Sanger			

Booker T. Washington			
W.E.B. DuBois			
Gifford Pinchot			
John Muir			
Theodore Roosevelt			
Woodrow Wilson			

22

WORLD WAR I, 1914—1920

SURVEY

Chapter Overview: This chapter covers the more active foreign policy of the progressive presidents Roosevelt, Taft and Wilson. America became more interventionist in the western hemisphere but when war broke out in Europe in 1914, most Americans did not see any national interest at stake. Loyalties were divided but eventually the U.S. joined the Allies when Germany broke its pledge on submarine warfare. Americans mobilized rapidly, accepting unprecedented governmental control. A drive to mobilize Americans' minds led to domestic hostility and violations of civil rights. Wilson went to the Peace Conference in Paris with his Fourteen Points to establish a new international ideal but opponents in Europe, at home and Wilson's own uncompromising attitude defeated his plan. U.S. victory in World War I made it a reluctant world power. In the 1920 election, Americans chose Harding's "normalcy."

Chapter Objectives: After reading the chapter and following the study suggestions given, you should be able to:

1. Explain how vigilante justice in Bisbee, Arizona exemplified the issues and conflicts of American communities during the war.
2. Summarize the ideals and actions of the "progressive diplomacy" of Presidents Theodore Roosevelt, William Howard Taft and Woodrow Wilson.
3. Outline the chain of events through which America entered World War I and the imprint it would leave on American economy and politics.
4. Discuss the efforts of the American government to mobilize the minds of Americans at home and American soldiers overseas.
5. Summarize the war effort as the ultimate progressive crusade and list the organization trends that would result.
6. Explain how participation in World War I increased many existing social tensions in America and what implications this had for the future.
7. Describe the struggles of Woodrow Wilson in trying to project his progressive ideas to the world and to his own constituents.
8. Making Connections: Chapters Twenty and Twenty-One: explain the connection between American pursuit of empire, the progressive movement and the United States experience in World War 1.

QUESTIONS/READ

AMERICAN COMMUNITIES: Vigilante Justice in Bisbee, Arizona: What were the issues of vigilante justice in Bisbee, Arizona? How did this community show divisions in American society? How did the war experience affect those divisions? What did the vigilantes do? What were the four backdrop items against which this deportation occurred? How was that indicative of many American communities during the war? What illegal conspiracy did the vigilantes carry out? How did they justify it? Why was the IWW vulnerable? What did the army census of deportees show compared to Sheriff Wheeler's claim? How did President Wilson react? What effect did the war have on American citizens? Identify: AFT, IWW, Walter Douglas, Citizens' Protective League, Workers Loyalty League, Senator Red Sutter.

BECOMING A WORLD POWER: How did Presidents Roosevelt, Taft and Wilson contribute to America's role as a new world power?

> **Roosevelt: The Big Stick:** What was Roosevelt's "big stick" policy and what imprint did he leave on America's foreign policy before and *while* he was president? How did Roosevelt obtain the Panama Canal? What was the Roosevelt Corollary and in what circumstances did he use it? What policies did Roosevelt follow in China and in Japan? Identify: Philippe Bunau-Varilla, Open Door, Russo-Japanese War settlement, yellow peril, Root-Takahira Agreement.

> **Taft: Dollar Diplomacy:** What was Taft's policy of "dollar diplomacy" and how and where was it applied? What limits did this policy have and how did Taft wind up using a "big stick" approach in Honduras and Nicaragua? What was the neutralization scheme of Taft and why did it fail? What happened to the situation in China, to the Open Door, and to Japanese-American relations?

> **Wilson: Moralism and Realism:** What was the moral basis of Wilson's foreign policy and how did realism affect it? What did Wilson believe he could achieve? How did the experience in Mexico illustrate the difficulties of his policy goals? Identify: Francisco Madero, Victoriano Huerta, Tampico and Veracruz, ABC Powers, Venustiano Carranza, Pancho Villa, John J. Pershing.

THE GREAT WAR: What was the Great War and how did America become involved? What effects did the wartime experience have on America's economy, politics and cultural life?

> **The Guns of August:** What were the guns of August and what events led to that point? What caused unprecedented casualties in the war? Identify: Triple Alliance, Triple Entente, Franz Ferdinand, Marne.

> **American Neutrality:** What was the American neutrality policy and why was it difficult to follow? What actually happened?

> **Preparedness and Peace:** Why did Wilson advocate preparedness at the same time as neutrality? What was the issue with submarine warfare and German tactics? What were the *Lusitania* and *Sussex* incidents and what effect did they have on American policy? What pledge did the Germans make? What support and what opposition was there to preparedness? Identify: William Jennings Bryan, National Security League, National Defense Act, Women's Peace Parade, American Union against Militarism, "I Didn't Raise My Boy to Be a Soldier," "He Kept Us Out of War."

Safe for Democracy: What was the implication of Wilson's war aim: "Make the world safe for democracy?" What German policy brought the U.S. closer to war? Why did the Germans take this risk? What were Wilson's first moves against Germany? What resistance did he meet in the Senate? What was the Zimmerman Note and how did that lead the U.S. closer to war? What executive order of Wilson's in mid-March brought more conflict and more pro-war attitudes? What was Wilson's argument in asking for a declaration of war and what the U.S. was fighting for? What was the vote?

AMERICAN MOBILIZATION: What steps did the government take to mobilize ordinary Americans to support the war effort?

Selling the War: What organization did Wilson create to sell the war? How did the CPI go about doing this? What were the three major themes of the campaign? What were the consequences of this campaign? Identify: George Creel, unhyphenated Americans.

Opposition to War: What groups opposed the war? What groups that opposed war preparedness were won over by Wilson and how did he manage to do this? How was John Dewey an example of this change? What was Randolph Bourne's dissent? What was the position of the Socialist Party and its leader Eugene V. Debs? What happened to the Women's Peace Party? How did most feminists react and who was an exception?

"You're in the Army Now:" How did the government proceed to raise an army? How was the Selective Service Act set up to avoid opposition to a draft? What was the reaction to the draft? How did progressives set up the army according to their reform ideas?

Racism in the Military: What examples of racism were there? How did the treatment of African Americans in France compare to home? Identify: 369th U.S. Infantry.

Americans in Battle: What did Americans initially expect their role to be and why did they wind up in battle? What was Pershing's view of war? How many men did Americans lose in battle and to disease? How did that compare to the Europeans? Identify: American Expeditionary Force, Chateau-Thierry, Belleau Wood, Meuse-Argonne.

OVER HERE: What effects did U.S. involvement in World War I have at home?

Organizing the Economy: How did Wilson go about organizing the economy? What was the War Industries Board and how effective was it? What government department did Herbert Hoover run and what was his success? How was the Money raised to fund the war? Identify: Bernard Baruch, War Service Committees, Food Administration, Liberty Bonds.

The Business of War: How did American industry and commercial agriculture respond to the war? How profitable was it for these two groups? What was the wartime trend toward a bureaucratic state and greater federal presence? While some practices were temporary, what ones remained after the war? How did the infant radio industry illustrate this trend? Identify: Radio Corporation of America.

Labor and the War: How did the labor unions respond to the war? What was the policy of the federal government toward labor? What did Samuel Gompers and the National War Labor Board accomplish? What happened to the Immigration Act of 1917 during the war? What happened to the more radical elements of the labor movement and specifically to the IWW?

Women at Work: What effect did war production have on women workers? What was the Women In Industry Service and what did its director, Marv VanKleeck, try to accomplish? What happened to jobs for women at the war's end? Identify: Women's Bureau.

Woman Suffrage: How did the war advance the cause of woman suffrage and women's status in general? What states had woman suffrage and why was it mostly western states? What tactics did different women's groups follow and what effect did the more radical National Women's Party have? Identify: Carrie Chapman Catt, Alice Paul, Nineteenth Amendment.

Prohibition: What groups were behind prohibition and how did the war help passage of the Eighteenth Amendment?

Public Health: How did wartime mobilization bring greater government involvement with public health issues? What were the major issues? What was the government response to the influenza epidemic? How did expenditures on medical research compare to later years? Identify: Raymond Fosdick, Division of Venereal Diseases, Children's Bureau, Julia Lathrop, Maternity and Infancy Act.

REPRESSION AND REACTION: How did the war intensify repressive and reactionary actions? At what groups were these actions aimed? What were the results of the federal government's anti-radical campaign?

Muzzling Dissent: The Espionage and Sedition Acts: What were the Espionage and Sedition Acts and what dissent were they intended to muzzle? How did the federal government enforce the acts? How did the government encourage vigilante activity? Identify: Bureau of Investigation, Eugene Debs, *Schenk v. United States, Debs v. United States, Abrams v. United States,* American Protective League, operatives.

The Great Migration and Racial Tensions: What was the Great Migration and how did it increase racial tensions? How extensive was the great migration? Where did many African Americans migrate? What racial violence occurred in East St. Louis and Chicago? How did business and local authorities increase racist sentiment? What did many African American leaders feel would happen from supporting the war effort? What happened instead? Identify: James Weldon Johnson, NAACP, Judge Lynch.

Labor Strife: Why did the labor peace of 1917 come to an abrupt end by 1919? How did many people in America view the strikes? What strike did Governor Coolidge crush and what was his view of this type of strike? What tactic did Elbert Gary, president of U.S. Steel, use to break an AFL strike?

AN UNEASY PEACE: How did the war continue at the peace conference? Who were the Big Four? How did Wilson see the peace conference and how did things actually come out?

The Fourteen Points: What were the major elements of the Fourteen Points and what was Wilson hoping for in terms of progressivism? What was the most controversial element of the Fourteen Points? Identify: Article X.

Wilson in Paris: How did the European public greet Wilson and what was Clemenceau's reaction? How much success did Wilson have with his Fourteen Points? What action did the United States take in Russia? What was the center-piece of his plan? Identify: Pan African Congress, war guilt.

The Treaty Fight: Why was there a fight about ratifying the treaty in the Senate? Who were Wilson's opponents? Why did the President resist Henry Cabot Lodge's actions and what did he try to do instead? What was the result? Identify: irreconcilables.

The Russian Revolution and America's Response: What happened in Russia during the war? Who finally took control of the Russian government and what did they do in the war? What was Wilson's initial response and later response? Why did American troops remain in Russia until 1920? Identify: Bolsheviks, Lenin, Brest-Litovsk, Comintern.

The Red Scare: What was the Red Scare and what caused it? Who was A. Mitchell Palmer and what campaign did he conduct? How did he make use of wartime acts? What was the reality of Palmer's predictions? What was the legacy of his campaign? What effect did it have on the women's movement? Identify: red-baiting, 100 percent Americanism.

The Election of 1920: What did the results of the 1920 election reflect about American desires? What was the crux of Harding's campaign? How great was Harding's victory and that of the Republican Party? Identify: normalcy.

CONCLUSION: What were the various effects of the war on American life?

CHRONOLOGY: Apply the standard questions from p. 4 of the Study Guide

STUDY SKILLS EXERCISES

1. Study tip: If you have been following the study methods suggested, you have already noticed that this text has useful elements for surveying and reviewing: the outline at the beginning of the chapter, the conclusion, and the chronology. The chronology gives you events pertinent to the chapter as well as previous and upcoming events. Look at the Chapter Twenty-Two Chronology on p.716. You should look at the chronology when you are surveying the chapter. Much may be new to you but you should at least recognize by surveying the outline and chronology together with the title of the chapter, WORLD WAR I, that your main task is to understand the changes in U.S. foreign policy and the process by which Americans went to war. When you get to the review part of SQ3r, you should use the chronology as a review using the questions that are suggested in the Questions/Read section. History is a time organized subject and even if your professor does not ask dates on a test, you should still pay close attention to dates to give you sequence and help you comprehend the material. For example, you should note that the *Lusitania* sinking occurs in 1915. It was not the immediate reason that the U.S. went to war but the country did begin to lean more to the Allied side. In 1917, you can again see the various steps by which the U.S. went to war. As you read the chapter, it is easy to lose track of this. You might also look for little tricks called mnemonic devices to help you remember a sequence or list. In this case, the first letters of the main events leading to war are in alphabetical order: L in *Lusitania,* S in *Sussex* pledge, U in unrestricted submarine warfare resumed, and Z in Zimmerman note--LSUZ. This seems like a silly process but remembering sequence can help you puzzle out answers on a test even when they are not questions about dates.

2. Reflections:
    a. Imagine a debate between Jane Addams and George Creel. What would the issues and main points be?

b. If you were in Congress in April 1917, would you have voted yes or no on Wilson's request for a declaration of war? Why would you have voted as you did?

c. How would you have voted in the presidential election of 1920 and why?

3. Making connections: many Latin Americans today still resent American foreign policies and attitudes. Connect the material in Chapter Twenty on empire and the material in this chapter on progressive diplomacy and consider why this resentment developed.

4. Vocabulary:

vigilante, p. 643   polyglot, p. 655
consortium, p. 647   armistice, p. 656
stalemate, p. 650   repression, p. 659
antagonizing, p. 650   reparations, p. 667
propaganda, p. 652

5. Maps:
a. *The United States in the Caribbean, 1865-1933* (p. 647) Into what countries did the United States send troops? Which areas were United States possessions? What amount of property did American businesses control in Mexico in 1910? What was the U.S. involvement in Guatemala? What countries did the U.S. financially supervise in this period? What were the canal options and where was it built? Be able to identify the countries and islands shown on this map.

b. *The Western Front, 1918:* (p. 656) In what country did Americans see most World War I action? Know the locations and significance of Cantigny, Belleau Wood, Chateau-Thierry, Second Battle of the Marne, MeuseArgonne, St. Mihiel. Be able to identify the surrounding countries of Europe.

c. *Woman Suffrage by State, 1869-1919:* (p. 662) Which two states had woman suffrage legislation by 1875; by 1900; by 1915? Where were most of these early suffrage states located? What group of states did not ratify the constitutional amendment? Who was Jeanette Rankin?

RECITE/REVIEW

MULTIPLE CHOICE:

1. The issue that prompted the vigilante activity in Bisbee, Arizona had to do with
   a. IWW violence.   c. management-labor conflict.
   b. Palmer's Red Scare Tactics.   d. the Great Migration.

2. Which one of the following did NOT side with or make up part of the vigilante group?
   a. Citizen's Protective League
   b. local authorities and businessmen
   c. Workers Loyalty League
   d. AFL

3. Which one of the following presidents was NOT a follower of progressive diplomacy?
   a. Theodore Roosevelt
   b. Woodrow Wilson
   c. William Howard Taft
   d. Warren G. Harding

4. President Roosevelt used his "big stick" diplomacy to team up with native forces and foreign promoters like Philippe Bunau-Varilla in order to gain
   a. the Panama Canal zone.
   b. Open Door advantages in China.
   c. protection for the U.S. Fruit Company in Honduras.
   d. more power in Venezuela against Great Britain, Germany and Italy.

5. Which one of the following was NOT an area to which Roosevelt and other presidents applied the Monroe Doctrine corollary?
   a. Nicaragua
   b. Mexico
   c. Haiti
   d. Colombia

6. Which one of the following is the RESULT of the other three?
   a. Wilson withdraws support from Pancho Villa.
   b. Wilson officially recognizes Carranza's government.
   c. Wilson sends U.S. troops to Veracruz, Mexico.
   d. Wilson tries to isolate Huerta from any international support.

7. When the war broke out in Europe, Wilson declared that he would follow this policy toward both sides:
   a. neutrality
   b. open door
   c. dollar diplomacy
   d. preparedness

8. Although Wilson's policy meant the U.S. could trade with both Germany and England, in practice we traded most with England because
   a. of a British naval blockade on all shipping to Germany.
   b. of Germany's policy of surprise submarine attack.
   c. many Americans were biased toward English culture.
   d. the British promised to stay out of Latin America.

9. Which one of the following was NOT one of the events from February of 1917 to March of 1917 that prompted the U.S. to declare war on Germany?
   a. Germany resumes unrestricted submarine warfare.
   b. The Zimmerman note is discovered and revealed.
   c. Germany sinks seven U.S. merchant ships.
   d. German submarines sink the *Lusitania* and *Sussex*.

10. Which one of the following has the LEAST in common with the other three?
    a. Randolph Bourne
    b. Jane Addams
    c. Eugene V. Debs
    d. John Dewey

11. Which one of the following is NOT true of the African American experience in World War I?
    a. Most African Americans were put in the most dangerous combat positions.
    b. French friendliness contrasted with white Americans.
    c. Units were strictly segregated.
    d. African Americans generally supported the war effort.

12. The Supreme Court cases of *Schenck v. the United States, Debs v. United States,* and *Abrams v. United States,* all upheld
    a. restrictions on union organizing during World War I.
    b. the draft laws of the government during World War I.
    c. extreme wartime restrictions on free speech.
    d. local cases which failed to convict World War I vigilantes.

13. "There is no right to strike against the public safety by anybody, anywhere, any time" was a statement that won this governor national prominence:
    a. Herbert Hoover   c. Calvin Coolidge
    b. Warren G. Harding   d. A. Mitchell Palmer

14. The "Big Four" was a reference to
    a. the major points of Wilson's wartime peace plan.
    b. American victories at Chateau-Thierry, Belleau Wood and the Meuse Argonne.
    c. four "irreconcilables" who opposed the Versailles Treaty.
    d. the leaders of Britain, France, Italy and the United States.

15. Which one of the following is NOT correctly matched to the agency led?
    a. WIB/Bernard Baruch converts industrial plants to wartime needs.
    b. WIS/Mary Van Kleeck coordinates women's role in the war effort.
    c. NWLB/Eugene Debs leads labor in wartime cooperation.
    d. CPI/George Creel promotes the war to the American public.

16. The most controversial of Wilson's Fourteen Points was his idea of
    a. a League of Nations.   c. national self-determination.
    b. war guilt for Germany.   d. free trade.

17. Which one of the following was NOT a group in the Senate that opposed the ratification of the Versailles agreement?
    a. isolationist progressives   c. racists
    b. Lodge supporters   d. labor supporters

CHRONOLOGY AND MAP QUESTIONS:

18. Which one of the following did NOT occur in 1914?
    a. U.S. forces invaded Mexico.   c. World War I began in Europe.
    b. Panama Canal opened.   d. Root-Takahira Agreement accepted.

19. Which one of the following gives these 1917 events in the CORRECT order?
    (1) Race riot in East St. Louis, Illinois
    (2) Bolshevik Revolution in Russia
    (3) Zimmerman Note discovered
    (4) Selective Service Act passed
       a. 3,4,1,2   c. 3,4,2,1
       b. 1,2,4,3   d. 2,4,3,1

20. The Nineteenth Amendment, on woman suffrage is ratified in:
       a. 1910.   c. 1919.
       b. 1915.   d. 1920.

21. A German U-boat sinks the *Lusitania* in
       a. 1914.   c. 1916.
       b. 1915.   d. 1917.

22. The United Fruit Company organized the banana trade here in 1899:
       a. Cuba   c. Honduras
       b. Nicaragua   d. Guatemala

23. Which one of the following was NOT a Caribbean nation that the United States had financial supervision over until 1933?
       a. Costa Rica   c. Haiti
       b. Dominican Republic   d. Nicaragua

24. The majority of action American soldiers saw in World War I was in
       a. Germany.   c. France.
       b. Russia.   d. Italy.

25. The first woman elected to Congress was from the state of
       a. Massachusetts.   c. Illinois.
       b. Montana.   d. Tennessee.

SHORT ESSAY:

26. Why was the building of the Panama Canal such an important achievement for the United States?

27. Compare and contrast Roosevelt's and Taft's approach to diplomacy.

28. Describe the use of propaganda by the European powers during the period leading up to U.S. entry into World War I.

29. Describe the use of propaganda by the U.S. government in its attempt to "sell the war."

EXTENDED ESSAY:

30. How did World War I increase the U.S. government's role in the national economy?

31. Did women's roles in the wartime economy further the cause for women's rights? Defend your answer.

32. How did U.S. interests fare in the Peace negotiations at Versailles?

ANSWERS-CHAPTER 22

MULTIPLE CHOICE:

1.	c, p. 643	10.	d, p. 654
2.	d, p. 643-4	11.	a, p. 655
3.	d, p. 645	12.	c, p. 663
4.	a, p. 645	13.	c, p. 665
5.	d, p. 645	14.	d, p. 666
6.	b, pp. 648-9	15.	c, p. 658
7.	a, p. 650	16.	a, p. 666
8.	a, p. 650	17.	d, p. 667
9.	d, pp. 651-3		

CHRONOLOGY AND MAP QUESTIONS:

18.	d, p. 670	22.	d, p. 647
19.	a, p. 670	23.	a, p. 647
20.	d, p. 670	24.	c, p. 656
21.	b, p. 670	25.	b, p. 662

SHORT ESSAY:
26-29

EXTENDED ESSAY:
30-32

23

THE TWENTIES, 1920—1929

SURVEY

Chapter Overview: This chapter covers the many changes in American life in the 1920s. After the war, Presidents Harding, Coolidge, and Hoover continued to encourage a foreign policy that would enhance American capitalism. A second industrial revolution based on electrical power, consumer goods and new management methods took place. The auto age made profound changes in American life and housing patterns. Some areas such as agriculture, railroads, coal mining and textile manufacturing did not share in the post-war prosperity. A new mass culture defined by radio, movies, music, newspapers and advertising encouraged a kind of national community. Some groups resisted the changes to modernity and met with mixed results. The postponement of democratic promise continued to stir reaction in women's groups, in Mexican Americans and the "New Negro." Intellectuals tried to put into writing the alienation and doubts connected to headlong pursuit of material prosperity.

Chapter Objectives: After reading the chapter and following the study suggestions given, you should be able to:

1. Describe the structural changes in the American economy that developed in the 1920s and the effects those changes had on American life.
2. Explain how Hollywood movies and other vehicles of mass culture created a new national community.
3. Describe how the new media of communication reshaped American culture in the 1920s.
4. Summarize the continuities of the administrations of Warren Harding, Calvin Coolidge and Herbert Hoover in domestic and foreign affairs.
5. Summarize the areas of resistance to the major cultural changes of the 1920s.
6. Outline the efforts of various reform groups, ethnic groups and intellectuals to redefine their missions, reshape their strategies and reexamine the material direction of modern American society.
7. Making Connections: Chapters Twenty-Two and Twenty-Three: discuss the various connections between mobilization techniques of World War I and the experiences of the decade of the 1920s.

AMERICAN COMMUNITIES: THE MOVIE AUDIENCE AND HOLLYWOOD: **Mass Culture creates a New National Community:** How did movies and radio create a new type of community? What was the cult of celebrity? What did Hollywood represent to millions of Americans? Identify: Roxy, Charlie Chaplin, Mary Pickford, dream factory.

POSTWAR PROSPERITY AND ITS PRICE: What was the price of prosperity? What Americans were the most prosperous? The least prosperous? What crucial changes took place?

> **The Second Industrial Revolution:** What was the second industrial revolution and how did it affect American industry? What was the shift from producer-durable goods to consumer-durable goods? What caused the boom in the housing industry?
>
> **The Modern Corporation:** What were the characteristics of the modern corporation and its leaders? What three key areas brought success? What companies were the most successful and in what areas? What new trend developed in corporate policy making? Identify: Alfred P. Sloan and Owen D. Young, oligopolies, Great Atlantic and Pacific Tea Company.
>
> **Welfare Capitalism:** What was the concept of welfare capitalism and how well did it work? Where did they fail? Identify: American plan, open shop, union shop, closed shop, company unions, William Green.
>
> **The Auto Age:** What were the various effects the auto age had on America? What did Robert and Helen Lynd find in their study of the Middletown community? From 1913 to 1925 what were the time rate changes for producing one car on a Ford assembly line? When did Henry Ford introduce a more generous wage scale? What other changes did he make? What tactic did General Motors introduce? What was the ripple effect of the auto on other industries and on the economy in general?
>
> **Cities and Suburbs:** What changes developed in cities and suburbs in the 1920s? What was continuing with the Great Migration? How did cities grow and what were major examples of each? How did the automobile suburbs differ form earlier suburbs? Identify: Empire State Building, Houston.
>
> **Exceptions: Agriculture, Ailing Industries:** What were the exceptions to the post war prosperity and why was this the case? What areas of agriculture thrived and why? Why did the textile industry move South? Identify: Ida Watkins, Hickman Price, McNary-Haugen Bills, Gastonia, stretch-out.

THE NEW MASS CULTURE: What was the new mass culture that developed and what were the specific elements of it? What effect did mass media have on American life?

> **Movie-Made America:** How common were movies by 1924? What expansion occurred when they moved to Hollywood? What was the studio system based on? What did Hollywood emphasize and how did it expand themes in the 1920s? What did Will Hays say about movies and the consumer culture? Identify: Adolph Zukor, Samuel Goldwyn, William Fox, *The Jazz Singer,* Roscoe "Fatty" Arbuckle, Will Hays, Motion Picture Producers and Distributors Association.
>
> **Radio Broadcasting:** How did radio broadcasting start and how did it expand? Who paid for radio programs at first and how did it change? What shows did the radio-created national community listen to? How many families heard radio by 1930? Identify: KDKA,

National Broadcasting System, Columbia Broadcasting System, "The Amos 'n' Andy Show."

New Forms of Journalism: What new forms of journalism developed in this period? What effect did tabloids have on advertising? What was the significance of chains such as Hearst, Gannett, and Scripps-Howard? Identify: Walter Winchell.

Advertising Modernity: What new techniques affected advertising? What connection did the changes have to World War I? How did psychology affect advertising? What was the key shift in advertising and what are some product examples? What do your authors mean by calling advertising therapeutic?

The Phonograph and the Recording Industry: How popular was the phonograph and what effect did it have on cylinders and sheet music? How good were annual record sales in 1921? How did records transform American popular culture? What regional markets were developed? Identify: Carter family, Jimmie Rodgers, Bessie Smith.

Sport and Celebrity: What was the significance of sport and celebrity in the 1920s? Who was George Herman Ruth and how did he exemplify this trend? How did Ruth affect the game of baseball? How did the Supreme Court affect baseball? Identify: Grantland Rice, William K. Wrigley, Negro National League, Satchel Paige, Red Grange, Jack Dempsey, Gene Tunney, Bill Tilden, Helen Wills, Gertrude Ederle, Johnny Weismuller.

A New Morality: What were the components of the new morality? What was the image of the flapper and what was she in reality? In what way was she a continuation from an earlier period and in what way was she new? What sources were responsible for a more open treatment of sexuality in the 1920s? What do sociological surveys from the time suggest?

THE STATE, THE ECONOMY, AND BUSINESS: What continuities were there between state and business in the 1920s? What administrations supported this continuity?

Harding and Coolidge: What types of presidents were Harding and Coolidge? What types of scandals were there in the Harding administration and how was he involved in them? Who was Andrew Mellon and what policies prevailed under his leadership? Identify: Ohio gang, Teapot Dome scandal.

Herbert Hoover and the Associative State: What were the experiences and principles of Herbert Hoover and what was his idea of the "associative state?" What effect did Hoover's policies have on the concentration of wealth?

War Debts, Reparations, Keeping the Peace: What was the issue and linkage between war debts, reparations and keeping the peace? Financially how did America emerge from the war? What was the Dawes Plan and how successful was it? Who was Charles Evan Hughes and what were his policies? What involvement did the U.S. have in the world affairs even though it was not a member of the League of Nations? Identify: Five Power Treaty, Kellogg-Briand Pact.

Commerce and Foreign Policy: How did Republicans connect commerce and foreign policy? What was the role of Charles Evans Hughes? What countries were invested in? What companies went overseas? What was the policy of the U.S. in Latin America and what consequences did it have in Nicaragua? Identify: Pax Americana, Sandino.

RESISTANCE TO MODERNITY: What groups and/or areas resisted modernity? What forms did this resistance take and how successful were they?

Prohibition: What happened to the long campaign for prohibition by 1920? What was the Volstead Act of 1919? How well was prohibition enforced? What effect did prohibition have on organized crime? How much did drinking decrease and what group increased their drinking? Identify: bootlegging, speakeasy, Al Capone, Twenty-first Amendment, "wets" and "drys."

Immigration Restriction: Why was there a move to restrict immigration and what immigrants were the target of this restriction? How did Madison Grant in his work, *The Passing of the Great Race,* reinforce anti-immigrant bias? What effect did the war and the Red Scare have on immigration restrictions? What did Henry Ford add to the sensationalist mix? What were the restrictions embodied in the 1921 Immigration Act and the Johnson-Reed Immigration Act of 1924? What groups did quota laws exclude? Identify: new immigrants, American Protective Association, Immigration Restriction League, 100 percent American, Albert Johnson.

The Ku Klux Klan: What caused the resurgence of the Ku Klux Klan? How did it expand its scope and use new techniques of communication? How did the Klan present itself? Where and when was it the most powerful? What were the various reasons it lost influence? Identify: *The Birth of a Nation,* "Native, White, Protestant Supremacy."

Religious Fundamentalism: What was the nature of the fundamentalist revival in the 1920s? What was a special target of fundamentalists? What were the issues in the Scopes trial? Who were the major personalities? What was the outcome?

PROMISES POSTPONED: What promises were postponed and what strategies did the groups affected turn to? How successful were they?

Feminism in Transition: Why was feminism in transition after the achievement of suffrage? What splits occurred in the movement? How did the League of Women Voters and the National Woman's party illustrate this split? What was the ERA and why did some women's groups and leaders like Florence Kelley oppose it? How did women's work change in the 1920s and what were the gains and losses? What was the 1921 Sheppard-Towner Act? What happened to it and why? Identify: politicized domesticity, Alice Paul, Mary Anderson, Amelia Earhart.

Mexican Immigration: How extensive was Mexican immigration in the 1920s? What encouraged this influx? What was the difference between this immigration wave and previous Mexican immigrants? Where did most of the new immigrants settle? What ambivalence did Mexicans feel about American citizenship? Identify: barrios, "greaser," "wetback," *mutualistas,* Federation of Mexican Workers Unions, League of United Latin American Citizens.

The "New Negro:" What was the "New Negro" and what did African American writers mean by this phrase? Where was the cultural capital of black America and what did it symbolize? What was the political side to the "New Negro?" What was the significance of Marcus Garvey and his Universal Negro Improvement Association? What was the white connection to Harlem? Identify: Langston Hughes, Harlem Renaissance, Claude McKay, Zora Neale Hurston, Jessie Fauset, Countee Collun, James Weldon Johnson, Paul Robeson, Bessie Smith, A. Philip Randolph.

Intellectuals and Alienation: To what extent were intellectuals of the 1920s alienated? How generally true was this notion? What ideas did Ernest Hemingway, F. Scott Fitzgerald, H.L. Mencken and Sinclair Lewis express in their writings? In the theater and in poetry, what ideas were discussed and explored by Eugene O'Neill, T.S. Eliot, and Ezra Pound? Who were the Fugitives and what views did they express? What were the views of those who were not alienated such as John Dewey? What were the views of Walter Lippman in his *A Preface to Morals?* Identify: lost generation, *The Sun Also Rises,* Jazz Age, *The Great Gatsby,* Babbitt.

The Election of 1928: Why was the election of 1928 a referendum on the Republican "new age?" What were the results and what did it reveal? Who was Al Smith and how did he personify the city and the immigrant? What did Herbert Hoover personify? What was his idea of "spiritual individualism?" Why did Smith himself become the main issue of the campaign? What areas did Hoover carry in the election and what areas did Smith carry? What was the significance of Smith's area of strength?

CONCLUSION: What was the status of America in the 1920s?

CHRONOLOGY: Apply the standard questions from p. 4 of the Study Guide.

STUDY SKILLS EXERCISES

1. Reflection:
   a. Imagine yourself attending the opening of the new Roxy Theater or one of the other movie palaces in the 1920s. How do you think you would feel?
   b. How would you have voted in the 1928 election? What issues would have been important?
   c. If you could choose one of the new career fields of the 1920s, which one would you choose and why?
   d. Commentators have argued that the 1920s and the 1980s were similar. Would you agree?
2. Making Connections:
   a. Connect the idea of the "New Negro" to the return of black soldiers from World War I, and to Marcus Garvey's black pride.
   b. If your class began with the Reconstruction Period (Chapter 17), what similarities do you see between the aftermath of the Civil War and the Great War?

3. Vocabulary:

celluloid, p. 677	normative, p. 687
durables, p. 679	crony, p. 689
synthetic, p. 682	autocratic, p. 692
moguls, p. 682	nativism, p. 695
minstrel, p. 684	alienation, p. 703

4. Maps:
   a. *Black Population, 1920*: (p. 700) What northern cities drew the greatest numbers of African Americans? How many African Americans were there in the North as compared to the South? What were the largest southern cities in terms of black population in 1920?
   b. *Election of 1928*: (p. 703) What states did Democratic candidate Al Smith manage to carry? In what other type of area did he run well? How effectively did Hoover win?

RECITE/REVIEW

MULTIPLE CHOICE:

1. Which one of the following was not part of the Hollywood "dream factory?"
   a. possibility of material success
   b. a chance to remake one's very identity
   c. the possibility of upward mobility
   d. great social authority

2. Steam was to the first Industrial Revolution as THIS was to the second one:
   a. coal
   b. electricity
   c. oil
   d. gasoline

3. The corporate attempt to improve worker well-being and morale in order to challenge the power and appeal of trade unions was known as
   a. American plan.
   b. associative state.
   c. welfare capitalism.
   d. oligopoly.

4. Cities like Houston, Los Angeles, Miami and San Diego all shared this in common in the 1920s:
   a. They were automobile suburbs.
   b. They expanded horizontally as their population grew.
   c. The Great Migration of African Americans concentrated there.
   d. Textile manufacturers from the New England states moved there.

5. Which one of the following was NOT true of farming in the 1920s?
   a. Farmers in citrus, dairy, truck and corporate wheatlands thrived.
   b. Tenant farming decreased as agricultural laborers left for the cities.
   c. Net farm income and land values dropped compared to the war years.
   d. American farmers had stiffer competition from overseas agriculture.

6. Warner Brother made a huge hit by bringing out the first "talkie," which was
   a. *The Birth of a Nation.*
   b. *The Love of Sunya.*
   c. *The Jazz Singer*
   d. *Amos and Andy.*

7. Walter Winchell typified the 1920s new popularity of
   a. tabloid gossip.   c. Hollywood stars.
   b. radio announcers.   d. sports writers.

8. Advertising of the 1920s paid most attention to THIS aspect:
   a. price of the product   c. quality of product
   b. U.S.A. made   d. needs of consumer

9. Gene Tunney, Gertrude Ederle, Satchel Paige, and Bill Tilden all illustrate the new celebrity of
   a. sports heroes.   c. sports writers.
   b. radio announcers.   d. radio stars.

10. The Teapot Dome Scandal involved questionable federal involvement on the part of Interior Secretary Albert Fall in leasing
    a. national forests to lumber companies.
    b. navy oil reserves to oil developers.
    c. federal facilities and vehicles to Prohibition violators.
    d. buildings and supplies for the Veterans Bureau.

11. As Secretary of Commerce in the Coolidge Administration, Herbert Hoover worked with Chicago banker Dawes on a plan to aid the recovery of
    a. tenant farmers.   c. the German economy.
    b. revolutionary China.   d. Central American countries.

12. Although consumption of alcohol per capital did decrease overall during Prohibition, it increased in this group:
    a. Bohemian radicals   c. Lost Generation writers
    b. working class immigrants   d. youth and college students

13. The "new immigrants" from 1890 to 1920 referred to
    a. African Americans migrating from the South to the North.
    b. Mexican laborers, both legal and illegal.
    c. Southern and Eastern Europeans.
    d. Asians from the Philippines and Japan.

14. Which one of the following was NOT a group to which the revived Ku Klux Klan expanded their hostility?
    a. Protestants   c. Catholics
    b. Jews   d. Darwinists

15. Which one of the following would have been the LEAST likely to promote the idea of politicized domesticity?
    a. League of Women Voters   c. Women's Trade Union League
    b. National Women's Party   d. National Consumers League

16. Writers Langston Hughes, Zora Neale Hurston, James Weldon Johnson and others belonged to a 1920s group called the
    a. Lost Generation of expatriate writers.
    b. Fugitives from the South.
    c. New Negro of the Harlem Renaissance.
    d. Ohio gang.

17. Which one of the following groups would have been the LEAST likely to vote for Al Smith in the 1928 election?
    a. American Protective Association
    b. a person against prohibition
    c. Brotherhood of Sleeping Car Porters
    d. newer immigrant groups

CHRONOLOGY AND MAP QUESTIONS:

18. The Equal Rights Amendment was first introduced to Congress in
    a. 1920.   c. 1926.
    b. 1923.   d. 1928.

19. Robert and Helen Lynd publish their classic community study, *Middletown,* in
    a. 1923.   c. 1927.
    b. 1925.   d. 1929.

20. Which one of the following does NOT happen in 1927?
    a. Scopes trial proceeds.   c. Lindbergh solos Atlantic.
    b. *The Jazz Singer* is shown.   d. McNary-Haugen Farm bill vetoed.

21. Which one of the following was NOT among the southern cities having the highest African American population in 1920?
    a. New Orleans   c. Miami
    b. Birmingham   d. Atlanta

22. The only area that was a strong showing for Al Smith in the 1928 presidential election was in the
    a. largest cities and the Deep South.
    b. Midwest and Great Plains.
    c. Pacific coast and Northwest.
    d. rural areas of the West.

SHORT ESSAY:

23. What is meant by the term the "Second Industrial Revolution?"

24. How did the automobile affect American society?

25. How did Hollywood "censor itself" in the face of calls for government censorship of the film-making industry?

26. How did "Babe" Ruth repair baseball's image after the "Black Sox" scandal.

EXTENDED ESSAY:

27. In what ways did sex and sensuality take a more obvious role in the culture of the 1920s?

28. In what ways was science misused to support the dominant racist theories of the time?

29. Were the twenties really "roaring" for all Americans? Defend your answer with specific examples.

ANSWERS-CHAPTER 23

MULTIPLE CHOICE:

1. d, p. 674-5	7. a, p. 684	13. c, p. 693
2. b, p. 676	8. d, p. 685	14. a, p. 694-5
3. c, p. 678	9. a, p. 686-7	15. b, p. 697
4. b, p. 680-1	10. b, p. 689	16. c, p. 701
5. b, p. 681	11. c, p. 690	17. a, p. 703
6. c, p. 683	12. d, p. 693	

CHRONOLOGY AND MAP QUESTIONS:

18. b, p. 704	20. a, p. 704	22. a, p. 703
19. d, p. 704	21. c, p. 700	

SHORT ESSAY:
23-26

EXTENDED ESSAY:
27-29

24

THE GREAT DEPRESSION AND THE NEW DEAL, 1929—1940

SURVEY

Chapter Overview: This chapter covers the cumulative effect of underlying weaknesses of the economy and the stock market crash that led to the Depression. Many unemployed workers blamed themselves rather than the system but more began to look to the government for some relief. President Hoover's response was consistent with his stated views but many began to demand more action and elected Democratic reformer, Franklin Delano Roosevelt. His first New Deal was a cooperative business-government venture but in his second he made a more dramatic shift, although not to the radicalism some critics accused him of. Other critics said he was not radical enough. Roosevelt's own ability to inspire, the activism of his wife and the action-oriented programs regained American confidence even though this did not end the Depression. FDR's impatience with the Supreme Court and his attempt to pack it cost him some political influence. Deep poverty was not really touched by the programs and minorities did not make major gains but they did form a coalition of voters that supported the Democratic Party.

Chapter Objectives: After reading the chapter and following the study suggestions given, you should be able to:

1. Describe the power of community as exemplified by the Flint sit-down strike in 1936.
2. Summarize the reasons why the Great Depression occurred.
3. Describe the government responses under Hoover and Roosevelt to the problems of mass unemployment and other effects of the Great Depression.
4. Compare the first programs of Roosevelt to the second reform package and the changes that were labeled the "Roosevelt recession."
5. Outline the views of critics, both right and left, of Roosevelt's New Deal programs.
6. Summarize the legacy of the New Deal for various areas and people of America.
7. Discuss how American popular culture was shaped during the Depression.
8. Making Connections: Compare the Dawes Act provisions from Chapter Eighteen to the Indian Reorganization Act in this chapter.

AMERICAN COMMUNITIES: SIT-DOWN STRIKE AT FLINT: *Automobile Workers Organize a New Union:* What was the sit-down strike tactic and why did it happen in Flint? What new union did the workers organize? How did they develop a sense of community? How badly did the Great Depression hit Flint? Why was this strike especially significant? Identify: Federal Emergency Relief Administration, Works Progress Administration., Wagner Act, Women's Emergency Brigade, Battle of Running Bulls.

HARD TIMES: How hard were the "hard times" that developed? What caused the Great Depression? How did the Hoover administration respond?

> **The Bull Market:** What was the nature of the bull market of the 1920s? What weakness was developing within the market? How many Americans owned stock? What was "buying on the margin" and why was this risky?

> **The Crash:** What was the nature of the Wall Street Crash of 1929 and why did it happen? Why did few people expect a depression even with the crash? What was Andrew Mellon's evaluation of the slump? Identify: Black Tuesday.

> **Underlying Weaknesses:** What were the underlying weaknesses in the economy? Why is it inaccurate to say that the stock market crash caused the Great Depression? What were the causes?

> **Mass Unemployment**: What were the statistics of mass unemployment? What did it mean to be unemployed and without hope in the early 1930s? Which groups found it easiest to keep work?

> **Hoover's Failure:** What was Hoover's response to the Depression and its massive suffering? Why was his failure ironic? What did he say in his 1931 State of the Union address? What was his plan and what assumption was it based on? Identify: President's Emergency Committee for Unemployment, Organization for Unemployment Relief, Reconstruction Finance Corporation, Emergency Relief Act.

> **Protest and the Election of 1932:** What was the nature of the protests and how did they affect the election of 1932? How extensive was the Democratic victory in both the executive and legislative branches? Identify: Farmers' Holiday Association, Bonus Army, Douglas MacArthur.

FDR AND THE FIRST NEW DEAL: What was the connection between FDR's personality and the success of the first New Deal?

> **FDR the Man:** What was FDR's background and family value system? What personal experience did he have that transformed him? What political experience did he have before he ran for president? What achievements did he have as governor that made him nationally popular? Identify: Eleanor Roosevelt, Temporary Emergency Relief Administration, brain trust.

> **Restoring Confidence:** How did Roosevelt work to restore confidence in the economic system? What was his inaugural message? What steps did he take to restore the banking system and what success did he have? Identify: bank holiday, fireside chat, Emergency Banking Act.

> **The Hundred Days:** What was the Hundred Days and what legislation was passed during that time? What was the plan or blueprint behind the legislation? What effect did each act

have? What was the "priming the pump" concept? Identify: Civilian Conservation Corps (CCC), Federal Emergency Relief Administration (FERA), Harry Hopkins, Agricultural Adjustment Administration (AAA), parity prices, subsidy, Southern Tenant Farmers Union (STFU), Tennessee Valley Authority (TVA), National Industrial Recovery Act (NIRA), National Recovery Administration (NRA), Public Works Administration (PWA).

LEFT TURN AND THE SECOND NEW DEAL: Why did the Roosevelt administration make a turn to the left in the second New Deal and what was its success rate?

Roosevelt's Critics: Who were Roosevelt's critics and what was the position of each group or person? What did the 1934 election illustrate about the popularity of his critics versus Roosevelt and the Democratic party? What were the programs of the following people: Al Smith, Upton Sinclair, Francis E. Townsend and Huey Long? Who was the greatest potential threat? Why was labor a force to be reckoned with? What unions and areas led major strikes? Identify: Father Coughlin, "Every Man a King," Section 7a of NIRA, American Liberty League.

The Second Hundred Days: Why did Roosevelt push for a Second Hundred Days and what were the goals of this second program? What was the nature of each of these acts: Emergency Relief Appropriation Act, Works Progress Administration, Social Security Act, National Labor Relations Act, "the Magna Carta for Labor," Resettlement Administration (RA)? Identify: John Maynard Keynes, Rexford G. Tugwell, Greenhills and Greendale.

Labor's Upsurge: Rise of the CIO: How did the New Deal affect the upsurge of labor? What was the CIO and why did they pull ahead of other unions? Who were John L. Lewis and Sidney Hillman and what were their views about unions and membership? What was the sit-down strike? What groups did the CIO organize? How risky was organizing in spite of the Wagner Act? Who was Frances Perkins and what connection did she make between the new unionism and the New Deal? Identify: Memorial Day Massacre.

The New Deal Coalition at High Tide: What was the New Deal Coalition and how well did it support Roosevelt in the 1936 presidential election? Who was the Republican candidate and what was the platform of the party? What was Roosevelt's program? Why was the *Literary Digest* poll incorrect?

THE NEW DEAL AND THE WEST: What impact did the New Deal have on the West? What was the long range effect of New Deal measures in the West?

The Dust Bowl: What and where was the Dust Bowl? What caused it and what effect did it have on the population? What federal agencies attempted to relieve the distress and what other steps did they take? What long term conservation and land use patterns did the government encourage? What effect did this have by 1940 and how did World War II change it? Who were the "Okies" and what people made up this group? Why did they migrate to California? What effect did this have on Mexican writers? Identify: Drought Relief Service, Taylor Grazing Act of 1934, Soil Conservation Service.

Water Policy: What water projects and policies did the New Deal usher in? What was the original role of the Bureau of Reclamation and how was it expanded? What was the purpose of the Boulder (Hoover) Dam and what was Hoover's view of the public power aspect of it? What was the effect of the dam on the land as well as the Bureau of Reclamation? What were the human and environmental costs of the bureau's massive

water projects? Identify: All-American Canal, Central Valley Project, Grand Coulee Dam.
New Deal for Indians: What changes did the New Deal bring for Indians? Who was John Collier and what did he do to the BIA? What were his beliefs about dealing with Indian issues? What were the provisions and effects of the Indian Reorganization Act (IRA) of 1934? What were the various reactions of Indian tribes? What was the Margold opinion and how did the courts regard it?

DEPRESSION-ERA CULTURE: How was American culture in the 1930s shaped by the Great Depression? What areas of popular culture became more central to everyday life?
A New Deal for the Arts: What innovative programs did the New Deal apply to the arts? What areas of the arts were supported and what types of projects were encouraged? Identify: Federal Project No. 1, Lewis Hine, Federal Writers Project, Life in America Series, Hallie Flanagan, *Index of American Design.*
The Documentary Impulse: What was the documentary impulse and why was it strong during the Depression? What were the motives of various individuals? Who was Roy Stryker and what was significant about his documentation? What was the double vision Stryker described? How was it exemplified in John Steinbeck's *The Grapes of Wrath,* Margaret Mitchell's *Gone with the Wind,* Sherwood Anderson's *Puzzled America* and James Rorty's *Where Life Is Better?* Identify: pitiless publicity, Ma Joad, Scarlett O'Hara.
Waiting for Lefty: What did "Waiting for Lefty" mean and what did it imply generally about some artists' and intellectuals' confidence in capitalism? How large was the American Communist Party? How did Marxist analysis influence people to flirt with communism? What was the "Popular Front" and how did it affect left-wing influence? What was the Abraham Lincoln Brigade?
Hollywood in the 1930s: How was Hollywood affected by the Depression and what types of movies did people like? What types did Hollywood offer the most of? The least of? What were the values communicated by Walt Disney and Frank Capra?
The Golden Age of Radio: How much effect did radio have? How much did it grow during the depression? How did the Depression actually help radio expand? What older cultural forms were continued by radio? What types of series programs were the most popular? How was Roosevelt an example of radio's potential political influence? How significant was the radio for news coverage? How reliable was the news?
The Swing Era: What was "swing" and what was it based on? Who was Benny Goodman and how did he adapt and popularize jazz? What effect did the mass culture industry have during the Depression? Identify: Duke Ellington, Fletcher Henderson.

THE LIMITS OF REFORM: What were the limits of reform and how did they affect New Deal programs? Overall how effective was the New Deal in ending the Depression?
Court Packing: What was court packing and why did Roosevelt attempt it? What effect did it have on his political power? What New Deal programs did the Supreme Court declare unconstitutional? Which one did they uphold? Identify: *Schecter v. United States, Butler v. United States.*
The Women's Network: What was the women's network? What impact did the Depression and the New Deal have on women? What was the influence of Eleanor Roosevelt in this network? What type of First Lady was Eleanor Roosevelt? How did

women's unemployment rates compare to their employment in work relief programs?
Identify: *It's Up to the Women,* Ellen Woodward, Molly Dewson, Frances Perkins.
A New Deal for Minorities?: What impact did New Deal programs have on minorities? What was the observation of Clifford Burke about the Depression's impact on African Americans? Why did Roosevelt not make any overt efforts to combat racism? What was Eleanor Roosevelt's role? What gains were made? What was the "Black Cabinet" and who were examples of individuals on it? How did black voters respond?
The Roosevelt Recession: Why did Roosevelt slow down spending for New Deal programs and bring about recession? What did Roosevelt's advisors think? What strategy did they return to? What reform measures were passed?

CONCLUSION: What were the legacies of the Great Depression and of the New Deal?

CHRONOLOGY: Apply the standard questions from p. 4 of the Study Guide.

STUDY SKILLS EXERCISES

1. Make a chart of all the New Deal programs with their directors, their nature, their impact (constitutional questions or rulings, if any).
2. Reflections:
   a. How would you have voted in 1932, 1934, 1936 and 1938 and why?
   b. Imagine yourself one of Roosevelt's "Brain Trust" people. What would you advise?
   c. Imagine yourself as a Roosevelt critic. What would your points be?
3. Making connections:
   a. What practices were being established at the turn of the century in farming (chapter 18) that affected the development of the Dust Bowl? What practices established in the New Deal in farming and water policy still affect us now?
   b. What programs proposed by the populists (chapter 20) were enacted in the New Deal?

4. Vocabulary:

   economic crisis, p. 715   zeal, p. 734
   bull market, p. 717   fomenting, p. 737
   hoarding, p. 723   stereotyping, p. 742
   scab workers, p. 729

5. Maps:
   a. *The Election of 1932:* (p. 723) Which states did Hoover manage to carry in 1932? How did FDR's popular vote compare to Hoover's in 1928?
   b. *The New Deal and Water:* (p. 734) What states were affected by the Tennessee Valley Authority? What river was harnessed?
   c. *The Dust Bowl, 1935-1940:* (p.31) What states were affected by the Dust Bowl? Where was it most severe? What federal programs were there and what effect did they have on migration?

RECITE/REVIEW

MULTIPLE CHOICE:

1. The "Battle of the Running Bulls" referred to
   a. the sporting arena atmosphere of the bull market in the 1920s.
   b. the government's ownership of the cattle industry.
   c. labor strife at General Motors in Flint.
   d. Roosevelt's conflict with conservative Supreme Court justices.

2. When FDR became president, one of the first things he did to re-establish confidence in the economy was
   a. set up the Temporary Emergency Relief Administration.
   b. declare a four-day bank holiday to shore up the banking system.
   c. establish the President's Emergency Committee for Unemployment.
   d. have Congress create the Reconstruction Finance Corporation.

3. The Agricultural Adjustment Administration was set up on principles based on proposals made by this earlier group:
   a. 1900s progressives   c. 1890s Populists
   b. Patrons of Husbandry   d. American Socialist Party

4. The Public Works Administration or PWA was based on the principle of "priming the pump" which meant stimulating the economy through
   a. providing jobs and increasing consumer spending.
   b. making credit available to businesses, banks and industries.
   c. encouraging small businesses and self-employment.
   d. setting prices at 1909 - 1914 purchasing power average.

5. Al Smith was to the American Liberty League as Huey Long was to the
   a. American Socialist Party.   c. EPIC Society.
   b. Abraham Lincoln Brigade.   d. Share Our Wealth Society.

6. When militant union leaders John L. Lewis and Sidney Hillman pushed to form a committee within the AFL to study industrial organizing, their goal was to
   a. run their own presidential candidate for the 1936 election.
   b. set up unions of mass production workers rather than by craft.
   c. draw all unions together into one huge and powerful organization.
   d. persuade Roosevelt to enact more social reform programs.

7. This Kansas Republican and editor of the Emporia Gazette attacked the New Deal for building up the Federal Government and creating a "Great Political Machine" centered in Washington:
   a. Alfred Landon   c. William Allen White
   b. Al Smith   d. Frances Perkins

8. If you were a western voter in 1932, Roosevelt's support for this was significant in winning your political backing:
   a. Boulder Dam
   b. All-American Canal
   c. TVA
   d. Central Valley Project

9. Overall federal agricultural and reclamation programs probably helped this group the most:
   a. sharecroppers
   b. Indian reservations
   c. large-scale farmers
   d. farm workers

10. Under John Collier and the Indian Reorganization Act, the Bureau of Indian Affairs did much to improve Indian situations. The heart of the IRA and Collier's attitude was
    a. strengthening the assimilation programs of the Dawes Act.
    b. the Committee of Indian Reorganization (CIO) to lobby the Congress.
    c. preserving Indian history through the Federal Writers Project.
    d. to restore tribal structures and tribal power to Indian groups.

11. FDR's fireside chats and Charles Coughlin's Nation Union for Social Justice shared what in common?
    a. more leftist ideas
    b. potential power of radio
    c. wanting more federal activism
    d. populist/progressive mixtures

12. *Schecter v. the United States* was to the National Recovery Administration as *Butler v. United States* was to the
    a. National Labor Relations Act.
    b. Reclamation Bureau.
    c. Federal Theater Project.
    d. Agricultural Adjustment Administration.

13. Which one of the following is the CAUSE of the others?
    a. Federal Reserve System tightens credit policies.
    b. Federal spending is cut back especially in the WPA and farm programs.
    c. The Roosevelt recession worsens economic conditions.
    d. The Fair Labor Standards Act is passed.

14. While New Deal programs were less numerous by 1938, the Fair Labor Standards Act established this first:
    a. federal minimum wage
    b. credit card laws
    c. public housing construction
    d. closed shop

CHRONOLOGY AND MAP QUESTIONS:

15. Place these events in chronological sequence:
    (1) FDR is elected president for first time.
    (2) Sit-down strike begins at General Motors Plant in Flint, Michigan.
    (3) Twenty-first Amendment repeals prohibition.
    (4) Bonus Army marches on Washington.
    a. 1,4,2,3   c. 4,1,3,2
    b. 2,3,1,4   d. 3,4,2,1

16. Which one of the following does NOT happen in 1935?
    a. The Committee for Industrial Organization is established.
    b. The Second New Deal begins.
    c. Dust storms turn the southern Great Plains into the Dust Bowl.
    d. The Dawes Severalty Act is repealed.

17. This Act, which established the first federal minimum wage, was enacted in 1938:
    a. National Housing Act   c. Fair Labor Standards Act
    b. Wagner-Steagall Act   d. the New Deal

SHORT ESSAY:

18. What was the goal of Hoover's Reconstruction Finance Corporation (RFC)?

19. How did FDR attempt to restore economic confidence in the U.S.?

20. What was the impact on western life of the New Deal's water projects?

21. What was the "documentary impulse" of 1930s America?

22. Why did Marxist analysis become prominent during the 1930s?

23. Why was FDR fearful of taking on the plight of black people during the depression?

EXTENDED ESSAY:

24. Why, in retrospect, were FDR's attacks on Hoover during the 1932 presidential campaign somewhat ironic?

25. How did FDR's political opponents influence him during the second hundred days?

26. Were FDR's New Deal activities socialistic as many of his critics claimed?

ANSWERS-CHAPTER 24

MULTIPLE CHOICE:
1. c, p. 716
2. b, p. 723
3. c, p. 725
4. a, p. 726

5. d, p. 727
6. b, p. 729
7. c, p. 729
8. a, p. 733

9. c, p. 732
10. d, pp. 734-5
11. d, pp. 726, 740
12. d, p. 741

13. b, p. 744
14. a, p. 745

CHRONOLOGY AND MAP QUESTIONS:
15. c, p. 745
16. d, p. 745
17. c, p. 745

SHORT ESSAY:
18-23

EXTENDED ESSAY:
24-26

Chapter 24- Study Skills Exercise #1
Significant Legislation During the 1932 and 1936 Roosevelt Administrations

Name of the Program	Date	Director	Nature of the Program	Impact of the Program
Banking Holiday				
Emergency Banking Act				
Civilian Conservation Corps (CCC)				
Federal Emergency Relief Admin. (FERA)				
Agricultural Adjust. Act (AAA)				
Tennessee Valley Auth. (TVA)				
National Industrial Recovery Act (NIRA)				
a. NRA				
b. PWA				
Indian Reorganization Act (IRA)				
Resettlement Admin. (RA)				
Works Progress Admin. (WPA)				
National Labor Relations Act (NLRA)				
Social Security Act				
Soil Conserv. Districts				
Nat. Housing Act (1934-1937)				
Fair Labor Standards Act				

25

WORLD WAR II, 1941—1945

SURVEY

Chapter Overview: This chapter covers the American involvement in World War II and its effects on the United States. America began trying to ensure isolation by enacting a series of neutrality laws but as the war broke out in Europe and Asia, the U.S. gradually altered the neutrality laws. Even before Pearl Harbor, the U.S. was involved in conflict with Germany in the North Atlantic. U.S. policy was to deal with Hitler first but the Japanese attack on Pearl Harbor changed that. The U.S. and its allies were on the defensive until mid-1942 when the North Africa offensive, the Battle of Stalingrad and the Coral Sea-Midway victories slowly turned the tide. The war became a battle of production with the U.S. possessing the advantages. While the U.S. fought the war for democracy, some constituencies still had to fight for democracy at home. The home front involvement in the war changed the lives of many women, African Americans and Japanese Americans. As victory was in sight, the U.S. was the major world power and at the center of global politics. Leaders tried to develop a new foreign policy to face these changing conditions.

Chapter Objectives: After reading the chapter and following the study suggestions given, you should be able to:

1. Discuss the problems in American communities created by war time changes using the Los Alamos scientists as your example.
2. Trace the changes in American policy from isolationism to involvement in the war in Europe and Asia as well as reactionary critics to the policy.
3. Summarize the effects of the war on the home front including business, labor, the family and various ethnic groups.
4. Describe the effects the war had on men and women in uniform.
5. Outline the strategies needed to win the war in both Europe and the Pacific.
6. Explain what significant changes developed in the last stages of the war.
7. Making Connections: Compare the U.S. involvement in and effects of World War I and World War II in terms of foreign and domestic policies.

QUESTIONS/READ

AMERICAN COMMUNITIES: **Los Alamos, New Mexico:** What type of unique community was Los Alamos? Why did the United States try to develop an atomic bomb? What broader changes were mirrored by the Los Alamos community? Identify: Manhattan project, Enrico Fermi, Robert Oppenheimer, "the gadget."

THE COMING OF WORLD WAR II: How did the U.S. government and various American groups react to the impending war? How was that reaction affected by World War I experiences? How did the U.S. slowly become involved in World War II?

    The Shadows of War: What events foreshadowed the possible outbreak of war? Where did war first spread? How effective was the League in these early events? By 1938 what areas were held by Japan, Italy, and Germany? Identify: Fascists, Mussolini, *Lebensraum,* Rome-Berlin Axis, Munich Conference, *Kristallnacht.*

    Isolationism: What was isolationism and how powerful was the legacy of this view from World War I? What was the Nye Committee? What were the various views of Americans from polls? What groups and individuals were part of an organized opposition? Identify: *All Quiet on the Western Front,* Neutrality Acts, Norman Thomas, Keep America Out of War Congress, American League Against War and Fascism, America First Committee, Robert Taft.

    Roosevelt Readies for War: What was Roosevelt's view of the war? How did the war in Europe begin? What steps did the U.S. take at that point? From March to August 1939, how involved was the U.S. in the war? Identify: "quarantine the aggressors," Nazi-Soviet Pact, *Blitzkrieg,* Neutrality Act of 1939, Selective Service Act of 1940, Lend-Lease, security zone and defensive waters, Atlantic Charter.

    Pearl Harbor: What steps did Roosevelt take in the Pacific? What steps were taken against Japan and how did Japan respond? What were both the Japanese leaders and Roosevelt doing? What did the U.S. expect based on breaking Japanese diplomatic code? What did happen? What happened at Pearl Harbor? What other areas were attacked the same day? How did the U.S. become involved in Europe? Identify: Jeannette Rankin.

ARSENAL OF DEMOCRACY: How did Roosevelt set about making the U.S. an arsenal of democracy? What problems were encountered? How successful was it?

    Mobilizing for War: How did Congress mobilize for war? What was the War Powers Act and what kinds of agencies were organized under it? What happened to the size of government and how did that compare to the New Deal? What happened to the budget and defense spending? What happened to most New Deal programs? Identify: Supply Priorities and Allocation Board, Office of Price Administration, Office of War Information, Federal Bureau of Investigation, Office of Strategic Services.

    Economic Conversion: How was economic conversion achieved? What effects did it have on the U.S. economy? How did the U.S. win the war? What was the War Production Board and how effective was it? How rapidly did military production grow? How did defense production affect various regions of the United States? What was the effect of economic growth on small businesses and farms? Identify: Food for Freedom.

    New Workers: What groups were the new workers recruited from? Which group's work pattern was most drastically altered and in what way? What was the dual message to women? How did women feel about those jobs? Identify: *bracero* program, "Rosie the Riveter."

Wartime Strikes: What disparity produced many strikes? How frequent were strikes in 1941 compared to earlier years? Once the U.S. entered the war, what did the major unions do? How did unions gain through National War Labor Board policies? What were "hate strikes" and what was the result? Identify: wildcat strikes, John L. Lewis, federal anti-strike laws.

THE HOME FRONT: What types of changes developed on the home front during the war? How did these changes compare to the aims of the New Deal?

Families in Wartime: What happened to marriage and family patterns during the war? What strains did the war place on marriages and families? How did the marriage and divorce rate compare? What problems and solutions were there with housing, rationing, day-care, juvenile delinquency, schooling, and public health? Identify: "Share Your Home," latch-key children.

The Internment of Japanese Americans: What actions were taken against Japanese Americans? What did a State Department intelligence report find? Who was John L. DeWitt and what was his attitude? Identify: Issei, Executive Order 9066, internment camps, Japanese American Citizens League, *Korematsu v. U.S.*, Tule Lake.

Civil Rights and Race Riots: What activism was there for civil rights during the war? What was the "Double V" campaign? How did the president react? What was A. Philip Randolph's plan and how did Roosevelt react? What levels of racial violence developed and where? What points were expressed in Langston Hughes's poem and Pauli Murray's letter? Identify: Executive Order 8802, CORE, NAACP.

Zoot-Suit Riots: What were zoot suits and how did they connect to rioting? How did the riots start? What communities clashed in the riots? What part of their community did zoot-suiters represent? How did the city leaders of Los Angeles react? What did the Office of Inter-American Affairs try to do?

Popular Culture and "The Good War:" How did the war affect popular culture? What themes were stressed in music, film, comics, and fashion? Identify: International Sweethearts of Rhythm, "good war," Captain America, "Loose Lips Sink Ships."

MEN AND WOMEN IN UNIFORM: How many Americans served in uniform and what effect did it have on them?

Creating the Armed Forces: What was the state of the various armed forces before the war began? How many did the Selective Service reject? How did Generals MacArthur and Eisenhower symbolize differences in command? Identify: George Marshall, GI, battle fatigue, Eddie Slovik.

Women Enter the Military: What was the level of involvement of women in the armed forces? What women's corps were developed and which ones were the most popular? In what capacities did women serve in the military? What discriminatory practices were there and which ones were changed?

Old Practices and New Horizons: What old practices were continued in the military and which ones were changed? What was Stimson's view about a "sociological laboratory?" What was the rate of African American enlistment? What discrimination did they encounter? How were Japanese American soldiers treated? What "Americanizing" experiences occurred to many soldiers? Identify: 99th Pursuit Squadron, Charles Drew, *Nisei*, 442nd, *Twenty-Seven Soldiers*.

Overseas Occupation: What was the mixed record of American occupation? What factors caused tension with our allies, military and civilian?

Prisoners of War: How many Americans were POWs? How did American POWs fare in Europe and the Pacific? What was the Bataan Death March?

THE WORLD AT WAR: What was the U.S. strategy in Europe and Asia? How did Americans proceed to fight in the war? What advantages did the U.S. and its allies have over the Axis powers? What were the significant turning points of the war?

Soviets Halt Nazi Drive: How and where did the Soviets halt the Nazi drive? What weapons and technology changed warfare since WWI? What did Hitler not take into account with Soviet resistance? Why did Hitler invade the Soviet Union? What was the Soviet toll in battle compared to American? How had the Soviets turned the tide? Identify: Stalingrad, Kursk.

The Allied Offensive: What sea and air offensives did the Allies launch in 1942 and how successful were they? What areas did the enemy hold? Why did the Soviets want a second front? What did the Allies do instead? Identify: El Alamein, Operation Torch, Casablanca, B-17, Dresden.

The Allied Invasion of Europe: What strategic decisions did the Allies make in invading Europe? How successful were their drives? Identify: Sicily, Warsaw Ghetto, partisans, Operation Overlord, D-Day, Charles de Gaulle.

The High Cost of European Victory: What was the high cost of European victory? What was the Battle of the Bulge and how decisive was it? What happened to Hitler? Identify: Arnhem, Battle of the Bulge, Ruhr.

The War in Asia and the Pacific: What was the overall strategy of the Allies in Asia and the Pacific? What areas did the Japanese hold? How did anticolonialism help the Japanese at first and then work against them? What "island hopping" strategy did the Americans follow? Identify: Stillwell, Coral Sea, Operation Magic, MacArthur, Nimitz, Tarawa, Leyte Gulf, Okinawa, *kamikaze*.

THE LAST STAGES OF WAR: What changes in foreign affairs developed in the last stages of the war? How did this affect military decisions? Who were the "Big Three" and what policies did they establish? What did Roosevelt want to achieve?

The Holocaust: What was the Holocaust and at what groups did Hitler aim this? How was this reported in American news? How did some journalists and American public react? Identify: Patton, Eisenhower's view, Buchenwald.

The Yalta Conference: What principles were established at the Yalta Conference? What happened to Atlantic Charter principles? What was the "spheres of influence" issue? What did Roosevelt report to the public and to his advisors about Yalta? What happened to Roosevelt in April of 1945?

The Atomic Bomb: What was U.S. policy about use of the atomic bomb? Who was the president by April of 1945 and what was his policy about bomb use? What was agreed to at Potsdam? How did Truman view the Russians? What were both the military and diplomatic reasons for U.S. use of the bomb?

CONCLUSION: What was the human cost of World War II both military and civilian? How did this compare to World War I? For Americans, how did it compare to earlier wars? What Allied nation suffered the most casualties?

CHRONOLOGY: Apply the standard questions from p. 4 of the Study Guide.

STUDY SKILLS EXERCISES

1. Reflections: How do you think you would have reacted to the following U.S. policies in the World War II era?
   a. The Neutrality Acts
   b. Changing the Neutrality Acts to Lend-Lease and other programs
   c. Internment of Japanese Americans
   d. The policy toward Holocaust victims
   e. The summer of 1943 race riots
   f. Yalta and Potsdam
   g. U.S. development and use of the atomic bomb

2. Making connections: What was the continued struggle of African Americans against segregation from Reconstruction to the war years? What would be the answer to Langston Hughes's question, "How long I got to fight BOTH HITLER—AND JIM CROW?"

3. Vocabulary:

fascist, p. 750	internment, p. 765
entanglements, p. 752	conscripts, p. 767
espionage, p. 756	stevedore, p. 769
militant, p. 760	partisans, p. 775
animosity, p. 763	logistics, p. 777

4. Maps:
   a. *Wartime Army Camps, Naval Bases, and Airfields:* (p. 767) Where were most military facilities concentrated? What new areas were opened up?
   b. *War in the Pacific:* (p. 777) What was the extent of Japanese control by August of 1942? As you look at this map, why do you think "island hopping" was a wise strategy? Be able to locate: Pearl Harbor, Coral Sea, Midway, Leyte Gulf, Okinawa, Hiroshima, Nagasaki.
   c. *War in Europe:* (p. 772) Who were the Axis powers and what did they control at their height? Be able to locate: Stalingrad, El Alamein, Sicily, Normandy, Battle of the Bulge.

MULTIPLE CHOICE:

1. The Los Alamos Community was an example of a
   a. Japanese American internment camp.
   b. unique group of scientists working on war research.
   c. new training base built in the West.
   d. scene of zoot-suit rioting.

2. Roosevelt set up the bomb project because he feared that THIS country was working on it:
   a. Japan
   b. the Soviet Union
   c. Nazi Germany
   d. Fascist Italy

3. In a foreshadowing of what was to come, the Japanese army invaded THIS area early in 1931:
   a. Korea
   b. Okinawa
   c. Thailand
   d. Manchuria

4. This American opposition group to war was most well known because of famous personalities who were members: Henry Ford, Charles Lindbergh and Lillian Gish:
   a. America First
   b. Keep America Out of War Congress
   c. American League against War and Fascism
   d. Nye Committee

5. Which one of the following was NOT an action The U.S. took before its formal entry into World War II?
   a. meeting with Britain to draw up Atlantic Charter principles
   b. a lend-lease policy to Britain and the Soviet Union
   c. U.S. ships to shoot on sight any Nazi ship in U.S. "defensive waters"
   d. asking the League to "quarantine the aggressors"

6. The War Powers Act gave a great deal of power to this section of the government to carry on the war:
   a. Congress
   b. the President
   c. the joint chiefs of staff
   d. the secretary of war

7. The CPI was to World War I as THIS was to World War II:
   a. OWI
   b. NWLB
   c. OSS
   d. FBI

8. Langston Hughes's question, "How long I got to fight both Hitler—and Jim Crow," was given organization by the African American
   a. "2nd Front" campaign.
   c. "Double V" campaign.
   b. Victory Garden crusade.
   d. Arsenal of Democracy program.

9. The zoot suit riots were started by uniformed sailors assaulting youth from THIS community:
   a. Japanese American
   c. Mexican American
   b. Italian American
   d. African American

10. The Nisei 442 Infantry was to the Japanese American as the 99th Pursuit Squadron was to
    a. women.
    c. Mexican Americans.
    b. German Americans.
    d. African Americans.

11. This counterattack was the bloodiest single American campaign since Gettysburg:
    a. Stalingrad
    c. El Alamein
    b. Battle of the Bulge
    d. Okinawa

12. Roosevelt and his advisers followed this policy in relation to Holocaust death camps:
    a. It was propaganda similar to World War I fabrications.
    b. Total Allied victory was the best way to liberate camps.
    c. Civilian rescue would be employed to distract the enemy.
    d. Soviet troops were closer and could liberate the camps.

13. Although this policy was unspoken, the United States and Britain accepted this area as a Soviet sphere of influence:
    a. areas of Manchuria and Korea
    b. the Middle East
    c. Baltic states and part of Poland
    d. certain Japanese islands

14. While lower than other allies, the human cost of World War II for Americans was second only to
    a. the American Revolution.
    c. World War I.
    b. Vietnam.
    d. the Civil War.

CHRONOLOGY AND MAPS:

15. Which one of the following was NOT seized by Hitler from 1938 to 1939?
    a. Belgium
    c. Austria
    b. Czechoslovakia
    d. Poland

16. From 1935 to 1937, the U.S. tried to adhere to THESE in order to avoid involvement in a war as they did in World War I:
    a. Quarantine Acts
    c. Neutrality Acts
    b. Atlantic Charter Principles
    d. Lend-Lease Acts

17. Japan invaded China in
    a. 1933.   c. 1937.
    b. 1935.   d. 1941.

18. Roosevelt's executive order to remove Japanese Americans from the Pacific coast states
    to inland camps was issued in
    a. 1937.   c. 1942.
    b. 1941.   d. 1944.

19. While military facilities were in many parts of the U.S., new construction for World War II
    particularly benefited THESE areas:
    a. Midwest and New England
    b. U.S. territories in the Caribbean and the Pacific
    c. the Great Plains both south and north
    d. the South and the West

20. The Americans followed this strategy in the Pacific to avoid sustained battle for each and
    every area the Japanese held:
    a. island hopping   c. second front
    b. wildcat   d. Double V

21. If you were a U.S. soldier and part of the D-Day invasion, where would you be landing?
    a. Sicily   c. North Africa
    b. Normandy   d. Philippines

SHORT ESSAY:

22. How did FDR prepare the U.S. for another World War?

23. What role did women play in the U.S. war effort?

24. Why did FDR avoid allocating U.S. military resources to stopping the Holocaust?

EXTENDED ESSAY:

25. What factors led to the U.S. having the upper hand in the war in the Pacific?

26. How did popular culture aid in the war effort?

27. In what ways did the economic power of the U.S. help it to win World War II?

ANSWERS-CHAPTER 25

MULTIPLE CHOICE:

1. b, p. 749	5. d, p. 752-3	9. c, p. 764-5	13. c, p. 779
2. c, p. 749	6. b, p. 756	10. d, p. 769	14. d, p. 782
3. d, p. 751	7. a, p. 756	11. b, p. 776	
4. a, p. 752	8. c, pp. 763-4	12. b, p. 778	

CHRONOLOGY AND MAPS:

15. a, p. 781	18. c, p. 781	21. b, p. 772
16. c, p. 781	19. d, p. 767	
17. c, p. 781	20. a, p. 777	

SHORT ESSAY:
22-24

EXTENDED ESSAY:
25-27

26

THE COLD WAR, 1945—1952

SURVEY

Chapter Overview: This chapter covers the beginnings of the Cold War under the Truman presidency as it affected both foreign and domestic policies. Peace after World War II was marred by a return to the 1917 rivalry of the United States and the Soviet Union. Truman and his advisors introduced the basic Cold War policies of containment in the Truman Doctrine, the Marshall Plan and the North Atlantic Treaty Organization. With the victory of the communists in China and the outbreak of the Korean War, America extended the Cold War to Asia as well. The Cold War prompted the U.S. to rebuild its World War II enemies, Germany and Japan, as counterweights to the Soviets. At home, Americans wanted to return to normal by bringing the troops back home, spending for consumer goods and re-establishing family life, but many changing social patterns brought anxieties. A second Red Scare was caused by the Cold War rhetoric of a bipartisan foreign policy and Truman's loyalty program, but Senator Joseph McCarthy's tactics symbolized the era. Defense spending increased and the American economy became dependent on it to maintain recovery. Truman tried to extend elements of the New Deal in his Fair Deal but with minimal success.

Chapter Objectives: after reading the chapter and following the study suggestions given, you should be able to:

1. Illustrate the effects of the Red Scare by discussing the college campus community after World War II.
2. Trace the development of the American policy of containment as applied to Europe and to Asia.
3. Summarize the foreign and domestic policies of the Truman administration.
4. Discuss the major causes, personalities and events of the Red Scare.
5. Explain the meaning of the Age of Anxiety and its reflection in American society and in popular culture.
6. Outline the events of the Korean War and its effect on American foreign policy and the political fortunes of Truman and the Democratic Party.
7. Making connections: chapter twenty-three and chapter twenty-six: compare the Red Scare after World War I to the one after World War II.

QUESTIONS/READ

AMERICAN COMMUNITIES: **University of Washington, Seattle: Students and Faculty Face the Cold War:** What happened at the University of Washington to Dr. Rader and the others? What was the Cold War and how did it affect the campus? Why were there record numbers of students on campus after World War II? How did older students view campus rules? Why did certain groups regard the campus as centers of "red propaganda?" What were most complaints actually about? Identify: Servicemen's Readjustment Act, loyalty acts.

GLOBAL INSECURITIES AT WAR'S END: Why did global insecurity exist at the war's end and what era did it actually date back to? What two powers were the center of power and why were they in competition?

The American Century: What was the idea of the American Century and who proposed the idea? What was America's position as a major military and economic power after World War II? Why did this success seem fragile to many Americans? What was the view of many businesses to ensure continued growth? How did the Soviets see the American Century? Identify: Bretton Woods, International Bank for Reconstruction and Development, International Monetary Fund.

Hopes for Collective Security: What hope was there for collective security? What did opinion polls show about American views of the United Nations? What were the General Assembly and the Security Council of the United Nations? Who were the five permanent members of the Security Council? What veto power did these powers have? What limited the UN and where was it successful? What role did Eleanor Roosevelt play in the U.N. and its programs? Identify: Dumbarton Oaks and San Francisco Conference, International Court of Justice, Nuremberg trials, Nuremberg Principle.

The Division of Europe: How did Europe get divided after World War II? Why was Roosevelt willing to accept a Soviet sphere of influence? Where did the Soviets gain control? Why did the USSR and France oppose German unification? How did Roosevelt's view about Germany compare with many American business leaders? What was Churchill's iron curtain? Identify: Yugoslavia, Albania.

THE POLICY OF CONTAINMENT: What was the Policy of Containment and how was it developed? How and where did President Truman apply the policy and how successful was it? What was Truman's view of the Soviets compared to Roosevelt's?

The Truman Doctrine: What was the Truman Doctrine? Where and why did he first apply it? How successful was the doctrine? How did Truman get public support for this doctrine? How did Congress respond? Who was George Kennan and what were his views on dealing with the Soviets? What was Walter Lippmann's view? Identify: Arthur Vandenberg, "X."

The Marshall Plan: What was the Marshall Plan and what was its aim? How successful was this plan? Who was Marshall and what was his reason for proposing the plan? How did the Soviets react? Identify: General Agreement on Tariffs and Trades.

The Berlin Crisis and the Formation of NATO: What was the situation in Berlin and why did a crisis develop? What was the nature of the crisis and how did NATO result? What was Operation Vittles and how did the Soviets respond? What was NATO and how did the Soviets respond? What was Senator Taft's criticism of Truman's policy? What did polls reveal about Truman's *taught line?* Identify: East and West German.

The Cold War in Asia: How did the Cold War in Asia compare to the one in Europe? What were the areas of conflict and the results of the Truman Doctrine in Asia? What policies did the U.S. follow in rebuilding Japan? What was our policy in the Philippines? What was the recommendation of Acheson in his White Paper? What was the Asia First group and what criticism did it make of Truman's policy?

Atomic Diplomacy: What was the implication of Atomic Diplomacy? What was Bernard Baruch's proposal to the UN Atomic Energy Commission? How did the Soviets respond? How did the military and scientists differ on the timing of the Soviets gaining the bomb? Identify: Atomic Energy Act, Bikini Islands, hydrogen bombs.

THE TRUMAN PRESIDENCY: What was the character of Truman and the Truman presidency? What themes did he follow and how successful was he?

"To Err Is Truman:" What were Truman's errors and what did he do to try to correct them politically? What was his public approval rating within a year of assuming office? What did Truman try to do in reconverting the economy and how did the public and Congress react? How did Truman try to revive the New Deal programs? How did Republicans try to turn back the New Deal and what particular group was their target? Identify: "Bring the Boys Home," Taft-Hartley Act.

The 1948 Election: How did various Democrats and Truman see the 1948 election? Who were the Americans for Democratic Action and what did they do? What was the difference between Wallace and Truman on views? What changes did Truman make on civil rights? What happened to Wallace's candidacy? What was the outcome of the election? Identify: Harold Ickes, Progressive party, "do-nothing Congress," Strom Thurmond's Dixiecrats?

The Fair Deal: What was Truman's Fair Deal program and how did it compare in ideas and theory to the New Deal? What elements of Fair Deal were enacted? How did the Truman administration use the threat of confrontation with the Soviets politically? What was the result?

THE COLD WAR AT HOME: How were Americans fighting the Cold War at home? Who were the "sides" in the war at home? What subversive activities were found? What was the result? Identify: Tom Clark, Joseph R. McCarthy.

The National Security State: How did the National Security State develop? What were the provisions of the National Security Act of 1947? What was Executive Order 9835 and how did Tom Clark carry it out? What groups were considered subversive? Identify: Pentagon, Internal Security Act, Immigration and Nationality Act, Subversive Activities Control Board.

The Red Scare in Hollywood: How did the Red Scare affect Hollywood? What was the House Un-American Activities Committee? Who were the "friendly witnesses" and the "unfriendly witnesses?" What was *Red Channels* or the blacklist?

Spy Cases: What spy cases developed and what were the events of the cases? How did the Democrats first see the Alger Hiss case? What was the role of Richard Nixon in these events? Identify: Whittaker Chambers, Alger Hiss, Pumpkin Papers, the Rosenbergs.

McCarthyism: What was McCarthyism? How many Communists did McCarthy uncover in the State Department? What did he accuse the Democrats of? To what extent did

McCarthy's ideas strike a chord? Who were his targets and how well did he succeed? What individuals and organizations helped him and who opposed him? How did McCarthy lose his popularity? Identify: Roy Cohn, showbiz, Millard Tydings, Margaret Chase Smith, Howard McGrath.

AGE OF ANXIETY: Why was this era called the Age of Anxiety? What did Americans do in reaction to it? How wealthy was the U.S.?

The Two-Income Family: What encouraged the development of the two-income family? How had the war affected the two-income idea? What group of women was seeking employment? What uneasiness did this create and how did some critics connect it to communism? What were the views of Lundberg, Farnham, Parsons, Spock and J. Edgar Hoover? How did the GI Bill affect women? What was the American woman's dilemma as stated by *Life* magazine? Identify: baby boom.

Religion and Education: How did religion and education respond to the Cold War uneasiness and fears of communism? Who was Billy Graham and what were his views? How did he view schools? What was the "Zeal for Democracy" program and how did it reflect the Cold War? What were the messages of historians such as Samuel Eliot Morison and Richard Hofstader?

The Cultural Noir: What was the cultural noir or mood? How was this reflected in films and books? What problems were there with symbols of prosperity? Identify: *The Best Years of Our Lives, Death of a Salesman, Catcher in the Rye,* UFOs.

END OF THE DEMOCRATIC ERA: What was the unresolvable dilemma that Truman faced and how did the trap of his own rhetoric affect the Democratic era?

The Korean War: How and why did the Korean War begin? How did the United States respond to the war? How did Kennan's view compare to Truman's? How did the Soviets regard the war? What effect did accusations of "selling out" Eastern Europe and "losing" China have on Truman? How did American citizens view our involvement according to polls? How did the first part of U.S. action proceed and what happened as MacArthur moved on? Why did Truman and MacArthur differ on views of the war? Why did Truman dismiss MacArthur? Identify: Inchon, Yalu River.

The Legacy of the "Sour Little War:" What was the legacy of the Korean War? Why did Truman call the U.S. involvement in Korea a "police action?" What was NSC-68 and how did it increase the power of the president? Who were the critics of this policy and what were the views? What was the end result in Korea when a settlement was reached in the summer of 1953? What was the symbolism of the movie "M*A*S*H," and its screenwriter Ring Lardner, Jr.? Overall, why was it a "sour little war?"

Truman's Downfall: What issue brought Truman's downfall? How did many people first react to MacArthur and what happened as Senate Armed Services and Foreign Relations Committee conducted hearings on his role in Korea? What did the hearings also reveal about Truman? What did Truman decide about running for re-election in 1952? Who were the candidates for the two parities and how did they compare in views? What was Eisenhower's program for ending the war in Korea? How did other supporters of Eisenhower criticize the Democratic candidate, Adlai Stevenson? What were the results of the election for both the presidency and Congress? Identify: K1, C2, Richard Nixon, Checkers speech.

CONCLUSION: What result did Eisenhower's election have for the Cold War? What was the "Eisenhower Movement" according to Lippman? What issues of the immediate postwar years seemed settled? What was the effect of Cold War defense spending? What happened to the sense of anxiety at least temporarily?

CHRONOLOGY: Apply the standard questions from p. 4 of the Study Guide.

STUDY SKILLS EXERCISES

1. Reflection:
   a. If you had been president at the end of World War II, how would you have responded to the Soviets?
   b. How would you have voted in the 1948 election?
   c. Would you have been in favor of the Fair Deal?

2. Making connections: Compare American foreign and domestic policy in the postwar 1920s with the policies of the postwar 1940s.

3. Vocabulary:

   disavowal, p. 786   proliferation, p. 805
   bilateral, p. 793   tandem, p. 811
   filibusters, p. 799

4. Maps:
   a. *Divided Europe:* (p. 794) What countries were in the NATO organization? Which ones were in the Warsaw Pact? How was Germany divided or occupied? Be able to locate or name all the countries shown here on the blank map.
   b. *The Korean War:* (p. 810) Be able to locate the 38th parallel, Inchon, Seoul, Pyongyang, Yalu River, and the Armistice Line.

RECITE/REVIEW

MULTIPLE CHOICE:

1. The main effect of Red Hysteria on college campuses was the
   a. restraint of free speech.   c. increasing radicalism of students.
   b. decline of enrollment.   d. increase in racism on campus.

2. Which one of the following would be LEAST likely to agree with the others on America's post-war role?
   a. Henry R. Luce   c. Arthur H. Vandenberg
   b. George F. Kennan   d. Walter Lippman

3. Which one of the following had the LEAST to do with trying to establish U.S. primacy in the postwar global economy?
   a. World Bank
   b. International Monetary Fund
   c. Council of Economic Advisors
   d. Marshall Plan

4. What did these five countries have in common: United States, Great Britain, the Soviet Union, France and Nationalist China?
   a. membership in NATO
   b. permanent members of the United Nations Security Council
   c. seats on the International Court of Justice
   d. members of the General Agreement on Tariffs and Trade

5. The Truman Doctrine was first applied to these countries:
   a. North/South Korea
   b. East/West Germany
   c. Turkey/Greece
   d. Yugoslavia/Albania

6. Truman was accused of "losing" this, of being treasonous, of giving a "white-wash of a wishful, do-nothing policy." This intense criticism referred to his policy decision on
   a. giving independence to the U.S. possession of the Philippines.
   b. failing to support MacArthur's views in the Korean War.
   c. breaking off relations with China's Jiang.
   d. atomic information in the Atomic Energy Act.

7. Statistically the national security state had 10 percent of federal employees before the war. After World War II's end, the federal work force in national security was
   a. 25 percent
   b. 35 percent
   c. 50 percent
   d. 75 percent

8. President Truman's Executive Order 9835
   a. desegregated the armed forces.
   b. brought combat troops home rapidly from WWII.
   c. ended the wartime price and rationing controls.
   d. established a federal employee loyalty program.

9. Which one of the following was LEAST likely to go along with the smear tactics of the Red Scare?
   a. Margaret Chase Smith
   b. Roy Cohn
   c. Joseph McCarthy
   d. J. Edgar Hoover

10. The GI bill underwrote these two items and caused a boom in both areas:
    a. federal employment and defense spending
    b. college education and housing
    c. automobile and television credit plans
    d. technical training and atomic energy jobs

11. The 1947 federal "Zeal for Democracy" program promoted strengthening national security and fighting Soviet communism through
    a. education.
    b. the family.
    c. women staying home.
    d. religion.

12. Which one of the following historians would have been MOST likely to have angered Joseph McCarthy?
    a. W.E.B. DuBois
    b. Samuel Eliot Morison
    c. Richard Hofstader
    d. Arthur M. Schlesinger, Jr.

13. An example of the age of Cold War anxiety was the popularity of the movie
    a. *They Live by Night*
    b. *I Married a Communist*
    c. *The Invasion of the Body Snatchers*
    d. *Red Channels*

14. As far as Truman was concerned, this Asian country and its situation was like that of Greece when he proclaimed his Truman Doctrine:
    a. Philippines
    b. China
    c. Vietnam
    d. Korea

15. The Korean War began when
    a. North Korea launched a military attack on South Korea.
    b. Communist China invaded Korea to keep the Nationalist Chinese out.
    c. the Soviet Union joined its North Korean ally in invasion.
    d. South Korea attempted to unify both occupation zones of Korea.

16. The Republican formula for attacking Truman and the Democrats in the 1952 election was K1C2 meaning Korea, communism and
    a. country.
    b. containment.
    c. Checkers.
    d. corruption.

CHRONOLOGY AND MAPS:

17. Which one of the following gives the correct chronological order of these events?
    (1) formation of NATO
    (2) the Truman Doctrine
    (3) Berlin Crisis
    (4) Korean War
    a. 3,2,4,1
    b. 2,4,3,1
    c. 2,3,1,4
    d. 4,3,1,2

18. In 1949 these two events occur that increase the Cold War anxiety of the United States:
    a. China becomes communist/the Soviet Union explodes an atomic bomb.
    b. The Soviet Union and China ally/the Korean War begins.
    c. HUAC hearings are held in Hollywood/the Soviets blockade Berlin.
    d. The Marshall Plan/Truman Doctrine are enacted.

19. Truman dismisses MacArthur and Armistice talks begin in Korea in
    a. 1950.   c. 1952.
    b. 1951.   d. 1953.

SHORT ESSAY:

20. Describe the major goals of U.S. foreign policy toward the Soviet Union in the years directly following the end of World War II.

21. What were the effects of the Marshall Plan?

22. What was the purpose of the House Committee on Un-American Activities?

23. Why did Truman feel compelled to act in South Korea?

EXTENDED ESSAY:

24. Evaluate the over-all success (or failure) of the Truman Doctrine.

25. How did the U.S. attempt to align western European nations with it against the Soviet Union after World War II?

26. What caused the economic problems that existed in the U.S. directly after World War II?

27. Analyze China's role in the Korean War.

ANSWERS-CHAPTER 26

MULTIPLE CHOICE:

1. a, pp. 786-7	5. c, p. 791	9. a, pp. 801-5	13. c, p. 808
2. d, pp. 788-92	6. c, p. 795	10. b, p. 807	14. d, p. 809
3. c, pp. 788-9	7. d, p. 800	11. a, p. 808	15. a, p. 809
4. b, p. 789	8. d, p. 801	12. a, p. 804	16. d, p. 812

CHRONOLOGY AND MAPS:

17. c, p. 813   18. a, p. 813   19. b, p. 813

SHORT ESSAY:
20-23

EXTENDED ESSAY:
24-27

27

AMERICA AT MID-CENTURY, 1952—1963

SURVEY

Chapter Overview: This chapter covers the changes in American society from 1945 to 1960. Although unevenly shared, America experienced great economic growth and affluence during the postwar era. More Americans owned homes, obtained college educations and experienced an improved standard of living. On the negative side, the cities declined, racism remained entrenched and the environment was damaged. A combination of public education, the baby boom and affluence helped create the youth culture expressed in rock 'n' roll. At the same time numerous critics objected to the development of mass culture of both youth and adults especially the headlong pursuit of material comfort. Both Eisenhower and Kennedy would search for foreign policies that would continue the leadership of America but met with mixed success. Eisenhower refused to challenge New Deal programs and even extended some. Kennedy tried to revive the liberalism of the 1930s with his New Frontier.

Chapter Objectives: After reading this chapter and following the study suggestions given, you should be able to:

1. Explain how rock 'n' roll helped create a new teenage community and define the nature of the youth culture.
2. Discuss the status of American society at mid-century and its major themes.
3. Outline the basic elements of mass culture as well as the substance of attacks by critics of mass culture.
4. Trace the continuing events and policies of the Cold War through the Eisenhower and Kennedy administrations.
5. Illustrate how the New Deal continued through both the Eisenhower and Kennedy administrations.
6. Making connections: chapters twenty, twenty-two and twenty-three: analyze and evaluate American policies toward Latin America.

QUESTIONS/READ

AMERICAN COMMUNITIES: Popular Music in Memphis: What variety of music was there in Memphis and how did it influence Elvis Presley? What type of music did Presley combine and what did he add to performance? How did the popular music called rock 'n' roll unite the young? What did the expression rock 'n' roll mean literally, musically and symbolically? What combination of factors helped the development of a youth culture? Identify: Beale Street, Midnight Rambles, Sam Phillips, Alan Freed.

AMERICAN SOCIETY AT MID-CENTURY: What was the status of American society at mid-century? What was the American public's view of the strong economic growth that followed World War II? How did this shape social life and politics? Identify: *The Affluent Society.*

The Eisenhower Presidency: What was the nature of the Eisenhower presidency? How did he view politics and political leadership? What was his view of a corporate commonwealth? What were the results of his approach for the environment? What New Deal legacy did Eisenhower accept? What were his views about pumping the economy through fiscal policy? What was the end result of his administration financially? Identify: Charles Wilson, Submerged Lands Act, Department of Health, Education and Welfare, Oveta Culp Hobby.

Subsidizing Prosperity: How did the federal government subsidize prosperity? What were the roles of the following programs in subsidizing prosperity: FHA, Veterans Act, Federal Highway Act and the National Defense Education Act? What types of negative effects were there in some of these programs? Identify: Levittown.

Suburban Life: What were the characteristics of suburban life? What happened to older urban areas? How did California symbolize the new suburban community? Identify: *The Feminine Mystique,* Norman Vincent Peale and Bishop Fulton J. Sheen, Centerless City.

Lonely Crowds and Organization Men: What points did critics make about lonely crowds and organization men? What were the major works and essential points of the following people: David Riesman, William H. Whyte, Sloan Wilson, C. Wright Mills?

The Expansion of Higher Education: How rapidly did higher education expand? What were the reasons for the expansion? What type of culture was predominant at colleges and universities?

Health and Medicine: What improvements developed in health and medicine after World War II? What changes occurred in physicians? Identify: National Institute of Mental Health, Jonas Salk, AMA.

YOUTH CULTURE: What was the youth culture and what caused the appearance of this group? What types of ideas and values drove the culture and what types of problems were there? Identify: teenager.

The Youth Market: What was the size of the youth market and what businesses pursued the market? How did this compare to earlier groups? How did public education increase the status of teenagers? How many went to school in 1900 compared to the 1950s? What was the overall effect of traditional adult authority paying attention to teens?

"Hail, Hail! Rock 'n' Roll!" What were the origins of rock 'n'roll? What was the role of radio? Why did it take white artists like Elvis Presley to exploit the new sounds and styles? What racial issues were involved in popular music? What was the significance of Chuck Berry? Identify: cover versions, Alan Freed.

Almost Grown: How were teens torn between youth and adulthood? What did the new teen magazines focus on? What things did they do earlier than previous generations? What is the significance of songs like "Sweet Little Sixteen," Yakety Yak," and "Summertime Blues?" What was sociologist James Coleman's observation?

Deviance and Delinquency: What deviance and delinquency developed? To what extent was there any real increase in problems? How did adults and teens differ on their views of rock 'n' roll? What is significant about these controversies in retrospect? What did Marlon Brando and James Dean symbolize?

MASS CULTURE AND ITS DISCONTENTS: What was the basic element of mass culture and how did it affect that culture? What did the critics say about these developments? How many people owned televisions by 1960?

Television: Tube of Plenty: How did television develop into a "tube of plenty?" "How did television compare to radio in its development and in its advertising? What were the staple shows of early television and how did they change by the 1950s? How did television affect movies? What unique ability did television have and what is one memorable example?

Television and Politics: What effects did television have on politics? What effect did television have on political figures like Estes Kevauver, Joseph McCarthy and Richard Nixon? What was the significance of the 1952 election to television?

Culture Critics: What were the ideas expressed by the culture critics? What two critics became best-selling authors and what were their works and ideas?

The Beats: Who were the Beats and what ideas did they express? Identify: Jack Kerouac's *On the Road,* Allen Ginsberg's *Howl,* beatnik.

THE COLD WAR CONTINUED: How did the Cold War continue under Eisenhower and what policies did he follow? What was his warning about the military-industrial complex?

The "New Look" in Foreign Affairs: What was the "new look" in foreign affairs and who developed it? How did Eisenhower feel about the new look and how did it get carried out with specific events? How did Congress react? What type of policies were followed by the new Soviet leader, Nikita Khrushchev? Identify: spirit of Camp David, U-2 flights, Francis Gary Powers, Sputnik.

Covert Action: What types of covert action did the United States carry out? Where and through what agency did the U.S. launch covert actions? Identify: Allen Dulles.

Intervening Around the World: Where did the CIA intervene and how successful was it? What problems did the U.S. have in the Middle East? How did the U.S. become involved in Iran, Israel, the Suez, Guatemala and Vietnam? Identify: Mossadegh, Riza Shah Pahlevi, Nasser, Aswan, Guzman, Ho Chi Minh, Dien Bien Phu, domino theory, Geneva Agreement, SEATO, Ngo Dinh Diem.

Ike's Warning: The Military-Industrial Complex: What was the military-industrial complex? What was Eisenhower's warning about it and why did he feel that way? What groups developed that protested the new look in foreign policy?

JOHN F. KENNEDY AND THE NEW FRONTIER: What were the views of John F. Kennedy and what was his New Frontier program? How successful was he in enacting the program?

The Election of 1960: Who were the candidates and what were the issues of the election of 1960? What was the impact of the televised presidential debates?

New Frontier Liberalism: What was the agenda of the New Frontier? Why was it difficult for liberal Democrats to achieve? What successes were there? How did Kennedy help revive the issue of women's rights? What was Kennedy's most lasting achievement according to your authors? What kinds of shift and patterns did Kennedy create in his presidency? Identify: Apollo.

Kennedy and the Cold War: What type of policy did Kennedy follow in the Cold War? What advisors did he choose in enacting his policy? What failures did he have? Identify: Special Forces, Alliance for Progress.

The Cuban Revolution and the Bay of Pigs: How was America involved in Cuba before the revolution and after including the Bay of Pigs? What was the outcome of the Bay of Pigs? Why did it fail? Identify: Batista, Castro.

The Missile Crisis: What led to the missile crisis and how did Kennedy handle it? What was the outcome and the other effects of the crisis for the United States and the Soviet Union? Identify: hotline, Limited Nuclear Test Ban Treaty.

CONCLUSION: What was the status of the Cold War at the time of Kennedy's assassination?

CHRONOLOGY: Apply the standard questions from p. 4 of the Study Guide.

STUDY SKILLS EXERCISES
1. Reflection:
   a. How would you have responded to rock 'n' roll?
   b. How would you have reacted to the critics of mass culture?
   c. What option would you have used in the Cuban Missile Crisis?
   d. What point of agreement was there between President Eisenhower and C. Wright Mills on the issue of power?
2. Making connections:
   a. What trends of the 1920s (chapter twenty-three) do you see in the 1950s?
   b. How much do you think Woodrow Wilson (chapter twenty-one) and John Foster Dulles would have agreed on foreign policy?
   c. What significant roles did Eleanor Roosevelt continue to play in the post war world? (chapter twenty-six)
   d. What points in this chapter do you still observe today in America?

3. Vocabulary:

cloying, p. 819	counterinsurgency, p. 841
locus, p. 825	covert, p. 841
array, p. 830	syndicates, p. 842
burgeoning, p. 833	chastened, p. 844
tactical, p. 837	

4. Maps:
   a. *Los Angeles Road System, ca. 1955:* (p. 824) What federal act encouraged the construction of freeways? What other development was connected to extensive road building?
   b. *The U.S. in the Caribbean, 1948-1966:* (p. 836) What happened to U.S. intervention in the Caribbean after World War II? In which countries did we intervene? What dominated U.S. policy after 1960? Compare this map to the one on p. 647 which covers 1865-1933. What countries was the U.S. consistently involved in?
   c. *Election of 1960:* (p. 840) Where did each candidate run the strongest? How did the popular vote of each candidate compare to the electoral vote? How close was the election?

RECITE/REVIEW

MULTIPLE CHOICE:

1. Which one of the following was NOT part of the significance of rock 'n' roll?
   a. It was an expression of common identity for American youth.
   b. It helped encourage a teen community.
   c. It demonstrated the new buying power of American teens.
   d. It accelerated a separation of white and black music.

2. This new cabinet post was created under the Eisenhower administration:
   a. Veterans Affairs
   b. Urban Affairs
   c. Health, Education and Welfare
   d. Defense

3. The National Defense Education Act (NDEA) was a bipartisan effort led by Eisenhower in response to the Soviet
   a. development of the hydrogen bomb.
   b. launching the Sputnik satellite.
   c. announcement of a manned space program,
   d. U-2 spy flights.

4. Which one of the following was NOT an item that increased from 1945 to 1960?
   a. mobility and rental of homes.
   b. numbers of people going to college.
   c. suburbs and centerless cities.
   d. disposable income of teenagers.

5. Television shows like "Father Knows Best" and "Leave It to Beaver" were
   a. about working-class families struggling with the dilemmas of a consumer society.
   b. about the real problems of postwar families who had survived the Depression.
   c. urban ethnic shows based on old radio programs.
   d. idealized, affluent, suburban, WASP, middle-class programs.

6. Walt Disney's *Davy Crockett* series was a memorable example of television's ability to
   a. ignore real-life problems.
   b. create an overnight fad.
   c. rework old movie themes.
   d. indirectly influence a presidential election.

7. Vance Packard's *The Hidden Persuaders* charged this group with exploitation:
   a. Central Intelligence Agency
   b. Television executives
   c. Advertisers
   d. Military-industrial complex

8. In his work, *Growing Up Absurd*, Paul Goodman argued that
   a. it was hard for young people to find a true sense of community.
   b. juvenile delinquency was on the rise in suburban areas.
   c. television was a cancerous growth on American culture.
   d. rock 'n' roll was the "devil's music" and "a communicable disease."

9. Eisenhower's Secretary of State, John Foster Dulles, called for a "new look" in American foreign policy which repudiated the
   a. heavy-handed interventionist diplomacy in Latin America.
   b. massive retaliation and atomic diplomacy of Truman.
   c. "spywars" and covert actions of the Truman administration.
   d. containment policy of Truman and Kerman.

10. When Nikita Khrushchev came to power, he made a goodwill gesture by withdrawing Soviet troops from
    a. Austria.
    b. Czechoslovakia.
    c. Cuba.
    d. East Berlin.

11. Eisenhower used the domino theory to justify America's
    a. military-industrial trial complex.
    b. containment policy in Asia.
    c. refusal to help seize the Suez Canal.
    d. covert CIA activity in Iran.

12. In the 1950s, groups like SANE, the Women's International League for Peace and Freedom, and the Student Peace Union conducted protests against
    a. the nuclear arms race.
    b. U.S. involvement in Vietnam.
    c. Eisenhower's refusal to stop the U-2 flights.
    d. Khrushchev's visit to the United States.

13. In its intentions, Kennedy's New Frontier originated from this previous program:
    a. Roosevelt's first Hundred Days New Deal
    b. Roosevelt's second Hundred Days New Deal
    c. Truman's Fair Deal
    d. Eisenhower's "dynamic conservatism"

14. According to the authors, Kennedy's most long-lasting achievement as president was his
    a. striking a resonant chord with American youth.
    b. strengthening of the executive branch.
    c. New Frontier program.
    d. insistence on a manned space flight program.

15. Eisenhower's choice of Charles Wilson as his secretary of defense and Kennedy's choice of Robert McNamara as his secretary of defense both illustrate
    a. appointing auto executives to run the government like a business.
    b. an opposition to the dominance of the military-industrial complex.
    c. a governmental reliance on Ivy-League college graduates.
    d. appointing former military men as advisors in government.

16. When Khrushchev pledged to withdraw missiles from Cuba, Kennedy agreed to
    a. withdraw missiles from Turkey.
    b. set up a hotline for instant communication between them.
    c. sign a limited nuclear test ban agreement.
    d. respect Cuban sovereignty and not invade the island.

CHRONOLOGY AND MAPS:

17. The CIA helped Riza Shah Pahlevi in Iran in
    a. 1953.   c. 1956.
    b. 1954.   d. 1961.

18. Which one of the following does NOT happen in 1960?
    a. Soviets shoot down U2 spy plane.
    b. John F. Kennedy is elected president.
    c. Bay of Pigs invasion fails.
    d. Almost 90 percent of American homes have television.

19. Rising star Elvis Presley signs with RCA in
    a. 1950.   c. 1954.
    b. 1952.   d. 1956.

20. The U.S. tried to buy it in 1869, sent troops in from 1916-1924, financially supervised it from 1905-1941 and then sent in the U.S. Marines in 1965:
    a. Cuba   c. Haiti
    b. Dominican Republic   d. Guatemala

21. The CIA-sponsored Bay of Pigs invasion of this country failed in 1961:
    a. Cuba
    b. Panama
    c. Haiti
    d. Guatemala

SHORT ESSAY:

22. Describe the factors that led to the expansion of higher education in 1950s America.

23. Describe the relationship between television and the advertising industry.

24. In what ways was television apolitical in the 1950s?

EXTENDED ESSAY:

25. Analyze how Eisenhower's pre-presidential career shaped his presidency.

26. Describe U.S. foreign policy during the 1950s.

27. Contrast the political backgrounds of John Kennedy and Lyndon Johnson and analyze how Kennedy's background influenced his presidential governing style.

ANSWERS-CHAPTER 27

MULTIPLE CHOICE:
1. d, p. 819	5. d, p. 831	9. d, p. 834	13. b, p. 839
2. c, p. 821	6. b, p. 831	10. a, p. 834	14. b, p. 841
3. b, p. 823	7. c, p. 832	11. b, p. 837	15. a, p. 841
4. a, p. 821-7	8. a, p. 832	12. a, p. 838	16. d, p. 844

CHRONOLOGY AND MAPS:
17. a, p. 845	20. b, p. 836
18. c, p. 845	21. a, p. 836
19. d, p. 845	

SHORT ESSAY:
22-24

EXTENDED ESSAY:
25-27

28

THE CIVIL RIGHTS MOVEMENT, 1945—1966

SURVEY

Chapter Overview: This chapter covers the mass movements for civil rights beginning in the black community and then extending to the Mexican American, Puerto Rican, Asian, and American Indian communities as well. This era, often called the "Second Reconstruction," saw advances against segregation through federal court decisions and more direct activism as black leaders forced the larger community to face segregation issues. The Civil Rights Act of 1964 and the Voting Rights Act of 1965 reinforced political equality but economic and social equality did not automatically follow. The persistence of poverty, entrenched racism and ghetto slums brought a split in the black consensus over goals for their movement. The civil rights movement overall and the Great Society created new pride and expectation as well as anger and a more militant movement.

Chapter Objectives: After reading this chapter and following the study suggestions given, you should be able to:

1. Explain how the Montgomery Bus Boycott drew an African American community together to challenge segregation.
2. Discuss the origins of the civil rights movement in the postwar years to the crisis in Little Rock, Arkansas.
3. Explain why and how some black leaders pursued means other than the legal strategy followed by the NAACP.
4. Summarize the successes of the civil rights movement from the Montgomery Bus Boycott to the Voting Rights Act of 1965.
5. Outline the issues and strategies followed by other minorities inspired by the black movement as well as improvements gained.
6. Trace the record of Truman, Eisenhower, Kennedy and Johnson in trying to change segregation.
7. Making connections: chapter seventeen and chapter nineteen: compare the first period of Reconstruction and the era following to *Plessy v. Ferguson* to the era after World War II with *Brown v. Board of Education* and a revived civil rights movement.

QUESTIONS/READ

AMERICAN COMMUNITIES: The Montgomery Bus Boycott: An African American Community Challenges Segregation: How and why did the Montgomery bus boycott begin? What was the role of the following people: Rosa Parks, Martin Luther King, Jr., E.D. Nixon, Jo Ann Robinson? What was the outcome of the boycott and how long did it take to achieve? Identify: Montgomery Improvement Association, Women's Political Council.

ORIGINS OF THE MOVEMENT: What were the origins of the civil rights struggle of the 1950s and 1960s? What various effects did the war have on civil rights during wartime and after? What were the early successes and setbacks of the movement? Who were its major leaders?

> **Civil Rights After World War II:** How did the civil rights movement gain its impetus after the war? What was the effect of the union movement on civil rights? What had the Truman administration done that kept the loyalty of the black voter? What happened to the growth of the NAACP in this era and what did they do during this period to challenge discrimination? What was the *Morgan v. Virginia* decision and why did activists begin the Freedom Ride? What was the outcome of it? What two symbolic firsts did Jackie Robinson and Ralph Bunche represent? What was "bebop" and what was the conscious design of this music? Identify: Adam Clayton Powell, Jr., Thurgood Marshall, Congress of Racial Equality.
>
> **The Segregated South:** What was the level and structure of segregation in the South? How many eligible blacks voted in the South and what measures were set up to keep them from voting? How did one black preacher summarize the difference between northern and southern white racial attitudes? What is the point of Paul Laurence Dunbar's poem, "We Wear the Mask?"
>
> ***Brown V. Board of Education:*** What was the background to *Brown v. Board of Education* and what was the aim or strategy of the NAACP in pursuing the legal case? What was Marshall's argument and how did the Supreme Court react? What happened when it came to enforcement and how did the second Brown ruling limit the effectiveness of the first? Identify: *Missouri v. ex. rel. Gaines, McLaurin v. Oklahoma State Regents,* Earl Warren.
>
> **Crisis in Little Rock:** What caused the crisis in Little Rock? What types of resistance were there to the *Brown* decision? What was Eisenhower's view of the decision and of his appointee, Earl Warren? Who was Orval Faubus and what was his role in creating the Little Rock crisis? What was Eisenhower's view of *Brown* and why did he take action against Faubus? What did Eisenhower do and what was Faubus's reaction? Identify: Southern Manifesto.

NO EASY ROAD TO FREEDOM, 1957-1962: Why was the road to freedom still difficult in spite of the Brown decision? What other tactics did the black community begin to use and what were their effects?

> **Martin Luther King and the SCLC:** What was Martin Luther King's background and what was the SCLC? What influence did Walter Rauschenbusch and Mohandas Gandhi have on King? What were the six key lessons King felt

were learned from the bus boycott victory? What shape did the SCLC envision for the struggle for racial equality? What happened instead?

Sit-Ins: Greensboro, Nashville, Atlanta: What was the sit-in tactic and what was the outcome in Greensboro, Nashville and Atlanta? What was the source of leadership in these protests? Who was Rev. James Lawson and what role did he play in sit-ins? Who were Julian Bond and Lonnie King? What was their role in the sit-ins? Identify: "Beloved Community."

SNCC and the Beloved Community: What was SNCC, how was it formed and what differences appeared in the black community over student militancy? Who was Ella Baker and what was her role in forming SNCC?

The Election of 1960 and Civil Rights: What was the civil rights position of each of the presidential candidates in the 1960 election? What happened in the process of the campaign? What happened when Kennedy became president? What changes did Kennedy make? Identify: minimum legislation, maximum executive action, Robert Kennedy, Civil Rights Act of 1957, Burke Marshall.

Freedom Rides: What were the Freedom Rides and what was their goal? Who was James Farmer and what was his role in the first Freedom Ride? What was the outcome? What other Freedom Rides followed and what publicity did they gain? What were the various gains of the Freedom Rides both in terms of Jim Crow and in terms of future struggle?

The Albany Movement: The Limits of Protest: What was the Albany Movement and what limits of protests did it expose? How did Laurie Pritchett, the police chief, deal with the movement? Who were James Meredith and Ross Barnett and what issue were they involved in? What did the University of Mississippi battle demonstrate?

THE MOVEMENT AT HIGH TIDE, 1963-1965: Why were the years 1963-1965 called high tide of the movement? What did they gain?

Birmingham: Why was Birmingham chosen as a place to launch a new campaign against segregation? What was the nature of the campaign? Who was Eugene Connor and what was his response to the campaign? What happened as the campaign was carried out? What significance did it have for building support and for changing the nature of black protest? Identify: Fred Shuttlesworth, *Letter from Birmingham Jail,* Freedom Now.

JFK and the March on Washington: What position did JFK take on civil rights and the planned march on Washington? Who organized the march and what was the result? Identify: George Wallace, Medgar Evers, A. Philip Randolph, John Lewis, Walter Reuther, King's "I have a dream" speech.

LBJ and the Civil Rights Act of 1964: What was LBJ's background on civil rights and what position did he take on the proposed legislation? What were the provisions of the Civil Rights Act of 1964?

Mississippi Freedom Summer: What was the Freedom Summer campaign and why was Mississippi the target? Who were Bob Moses and Dave Dennis and what did they expect in their campaign? What were the results? What tensions took place within the "beloved community?" What was the success of the campaign in terms of registration to vote and gaining national attention? What was the MFDP and what problem did it illustrate? Identify: freedom schools, Neshoba County, Ruby Robinson.

Malcolm X and Black Consciousness: What change in black consciousness did Malcolm X represent? What was his view of the civil rights movement? What change did he make later? Identify: Nation of Islam, Elijah Mohammed, *Autobiography of Malcolm X,* Organization of Afro-American Unity, Black Power.

Selma and the Voting Rights Act of 1965: Why was Selma the next choice for a campaign and what did the movement leaders hope would happen? Why was the Selma to Montgomery march the next step? What happened as a result of "Bloody Sunday" at the Pettus Bridge? As the Selma movement lost momentum, what happened to revive it? What were the provisions of the Voting Rights Act and what levels of registration were reached?

FORGOTTEN MINORITIES, 1945-1965: Who were the forgotten minorities and what effect did the black civil rights movement have on them? What did they gain?

Mexican Americans: What activities did the postwar Mexican American groups stress? What was the significance of each of the following court cases: *Mendez v. Westminster, Delgado case, Hernandez decision?* Identify: LULAC, GI Forum, *bracero, jojados,* "Operation Wetback," *la raza.*

Puerto Ricans: What was the relationship between the United States and Puerto Rico? Where did most Puerto Ricans go in the "great migration?" What problems did they encounter and what did their community concentrate on gaining? Identify: Jones Act of 1917, *el barrio.*

Indian Peoples: What policy change affected Indian peoples and how did it increase their activism? What problems were there on reservations? What was the BIA relocation program? Identify: "termination," House Concurrent Resolution 108, National Congress of American Indians, Native American Rights Fund, Indian Claims Commission, *U.S. v. Wheeler,* "ethnic Indians," National Indian Youth Council.

Asian Americans: What happened to Japanese Americans after the relocation program of World War II? What was the JACL and what did they manage to defeat in California? How did the McCarran-Walter Act and then the Immigration and Nationality Acts of 1952 and 1965 change citizenship and immigration patterns? What were the statistics of Asian immigration form 1960 to 1985?

CONCLUSION: **Free at Last?** What gains were made toward political or constitutional freedom? What was the central assumption of liberalism? By the mid-1960s, what changes were developing within black groups as well as white opposition groups? What was Martin Luther King's broader vision?

STUDY SKILLS EXERCISES

1. Reflection:
   a. Imagine yourself as a black living in the South in the 1950s. What activist group, if any, would have appealed to you? Imagine yourself as a white living in the South in the 1950s. What side would you take?
   b. What is the appeal of an idea like the "beloved community?" Is it possible to achieve?

2. Making connections:
   a. Compare the *Plessy v. Ferguson* and Jim Crow laws (chapter 19 and chapter 21) with the changes made by the cases leading up to and including *Brown v. Board of Education.*
   b. How did the Brandeis brief (chapter 21) help Thurgood Marshall?
   c. What are the similarities between the union tactic of the sit-down strike (chapter 24) and the sit-in tactic?

3. Vocabulary:

contingent, p. 850	mediators, p. 863
pivotal, p. 851	vigil, p. 865
epithets, p. 852	enjoined, p. 870
vilification, p. 858	chronic, p. 874

4. Maps:
   a. *Map of the Civil Rights Movement:* (p. 855) In general where were the key battlegrounds in the civil rights movement? Be able to match each of these cities to the significant civil rights movement events that happened there. Be able to identify or match the event(s) to the city(s). Be able to locate the cities and states on a blank map.
   b. *Impact of the Voting Rights Act of 1965:* (p. 870) In general, what happened to voter registration among African Americans in the South between 1960 and 1971? Which state had the LEAST percentage of registered black voters in 1960? Which state had the MOST? Which state was still the lowest in 1971? Which state was the highest in 1971?

RECITE/REVIEW

MULTIPLE CHOICE:

1. In 1955, the black community in Montgomery, Alabama represented this fraction of the city's population:
   a. one-tenth
   b. one-fourth
   c. one-third
   d. one-half

2. Which one of the following was NOT a step President Truman took that shifted most black voters to the Democratic Party?
   a. A presidential committee on Civil Rights that made ambitious recommendations.
   b. Truman publicly endorsed the report: *To Secure These Rights*.
   c. He desegregated the armed forces by executive order.
   d. He met with Thurgood Marshall and praised the NAACP.

3. Black jazz musicians created a more complex music in the forties that was harder for whites to copy, cover over or sweeten. This music was called
   a. bebop.
   b. rockabilly.
   c. rebop.
   d. swing.

4. A combination of legal and violent acts kept all but the most determined blacks from voting in the late 1940s. The number was—percent.
   a. one
   b. five
   c. ten
   d. fifteen

5. The victory in *Brown v. Board of Education* was limited by this second ruling:
   a. accepting the idea of "interposition" as a legal argument.
   b. giving responsibility for implementation to local school boards.
   c. monitoring would be decided by the local community.
   d. schools would have a ten year time plan to implement.

6. Martin Luther King, Jr. was inspired by this American theologian's social Christianity:
   a. Walter Rauschenbusch
   b. Ralph Abernathy
   c. Billy Graham
   d. Norman Vincent Peale

7. Greensboro, North Carolina, Nashville, Tennessee, and Atlanta, Georgia were the sites of this particular strategy of the civil rights movement:
   a. Freedom rides to test the *Morgan v. Virginia* ruling in interstate buses
   b. Mass signings of a Southern manifesto to defeat segregation
   c. Sit-ins at lunch counters and restaurants to protest discrimination
   d. Voter registration drives to increase the number of black voters

8. The Freedom Rides were to *Morgan v. Virginia* desegregation on interstate facilities as the Mississippi Freedom Summer was to
   a. voter registration.
   b. college registration.
   c. union organizing.
   d. job opportunity.

9. Which one of the following was NOT a crisis planned to arouse national indignation?
   a. Birmingham campaign
   b. Selma campaign
   c. March on Washington
   d. Albany Movement

10. Which one of the following has the LEAST to do with Malcolm Little?
    a. Nation of Islam
    c. Black Muslims
    b. Black Power
    d. "Bloody Sunday"

11. The Immigration and Nationality Act of 1965 ended
    a. termination policy.
    c. Operation Wetback.
    b. national-origin quotas.
    d. Issei citizenship eligibility.

12. The NAACP was to pursuing legal cases in the black community as THIS group
    was in the Mexican American community:
    a. LULAC
    c. BRACERO
    b. La RAZA
    d. ANMA

13. The Jones Act of 1917 granted U.S. citizenship to
    a. Issei.
    c. illegal Mexican immigrants.
    b. Puerto Ricans.
    d. Native Americans not on reservations.

14. With the change in the Immigration and Nationality Act of 1965, this group was
    not the largest Asian-American group in 1985 as it had been in 1960:
    a. Chinese
    c. Japanese
    b. Vietnamese
    d. Korean

15. Which one of the following court cases is NOT correctly matched with the topic of
    the decision?
    a. *U.S. v. Wheeler*: unique and limited sovereignty of Indian tribes
    b. *Mendez v. Westminste:* illegality of segregation of Mexican Americans
    c. *Missouri v. ex. rel. Gaines*: a separate law school must be fully equal
    d. *McLaurin v. Oklahoma State Regents*: black students must be admitted to law
       school

CHRONOLOGY AND MAPS:

16. Which one of the following lists the CORRECT order of these events?
    (1) Brown case rules segregated schools are inherently unequal
    (2) Executive Order 8802 forbids racial discrimination in defense industries
    (3) Truman issues executive order desegregating the armed forces
    (4) Morgan case rules segregation on interstate buses is unconstitutional
        a. 2,3,4,1
        c. 2,3,1,4
        b. 2,4,3,1
        d. 2,4,1,3

17. The Mississippi Freedom Democratic Party is denied seats at this presidential
    convention:
    a. 1952
    c. 1960
    b. 1956
    d. 1964

18. Eisenhower sent troops to integrate a high school in
   a. Selma, Alabama.
   c. Little Rock, Arkansas.
   b. Atlanta, Georgia.
   d. Oxford, Mississippi.

19. The Freedom Summer activists concentrated on this southern state since it had the lowest number of African American registered voters in 1960:
   a. Louisiana
   c. Alabama
   b. South Carolina
   d. Mississippi

SHORT ESSAY:

20. Explain the quotation attributed to a black preacher on p. 853.

21. How did the events at Little Rock High School define the role of the federal government with respect to civil rights?

22. What event thrust Martin Luther King, Jr. into the national spotlight and why? Describe King's involvement in this event.

23. Describe Lyndon Johnson's role in passing the Civil Rights Act of 1964.

EXTENDED ESSAY:

24. What is the irony of the role the civil rights issue played in the 1960 presidential election? Why did this irony come about?

25. Analyze the effect the black civil rights movement had on the movements to gain civil rights for other minority groups.

26. Compare and contrast the roles of Martin Luther King, Jr. and Malcolm X in the black community.

ANSWERS-CHAPTER 28

MULTIPLE CHOICE:
1.	d, p. 849	6.	a, p. 856	11.	b, p. 874
2.	d, p. 851	7.	c, p. 857-8	12.	a, p. 871
3.	a, p. 852	8.	a, p. 867-8	13.	b, p. 872
4.	c, p. 853	9.	d, p. 861	14.	c, p. 874
5.	b, p. 854	10.	d, p. 870	15.	d, p. 854

CHRONOLOGY AND MAPS:
16.	b, p. 875	17.	d, p. 875	18.	c, p. 855	19.	d, p. 870

SHORT ESSAY:
20-23

EXTENDED ESSAY:
24-26

29

WAR ABROAD, WAR AT HOME, 1965—1974

SURVEY

Chapter Overview: This chapter covers the Vietnam conflict, the longest and least successful war in American history. The period of the greatest involvement was from 1965 to 1974 and because of their policies, it became known as Johnson's war and Nixon's war. The war and actions against it diverted the domestic agendas of President Johnson and the student groups. Ironically President Nixon proved not to be as conservative as expected in some social reform areas. He was also able to make a major foreign policy change with China and subsequently with the Soviet Union. The civil rights movement spurred other groups from college students to gays, women, Latinos, Asian Americans and Indians. Both the war and the agendas of the various groups dominated the politics of both the 1968 and 1972 presidential elections. 1968 would be a turning point with the Tet offensive, which while won by the Americans, shocked the nation because of the gap it illustrated between rosy predictions of winning and actual fact. Martin Luther King, Jr. and Robert F. Kennedy were assassinated. The 1968 Democratic Convention would be surrounded by great violence. The national mood was dismal and the events of the Nixon administration and Watergate did not rebuild any national community consensus.

Chapter Objectives: after reading this chapter and following the study suggestions given, you should be able to:

1. Explain the spirit of community that college students and other groups were seeking in the 1960s.
2. Explain how the Vietnam War became Johnson's and then Nixon's war in spite of previous American involvement.
3. Trace the shift in the civil rights movement from King's leadership to the black power of Stokely Carmichael and others.
4. Discuss why certain events of 1968 were pivotal in American domestic and foreign policies.
5. Summarize the impact of the civil rights movement on other groups and outline the beliefs and agendas of these groups.
6. Summarize the domestic and foreign policies of the Nixon administration and explain how the Watergate issue brought it to an end.

7. Making connections: chapters 26 and 27: trace the involvement of the United States in Vietnam from the Truman to the Eisenhower to the Kennedy administrations and tie this into Objective 2 above.

QUESTIONS/READ

AMERICAN COMMUNITIES: **Uptown Chicago, Illinois:** What was the Uptown community and how did it illustrate the promise and problem of community in this era? Who were the Students for a Democratic Society and what type of agenda did they have? How large was the organization? How successful were their projects? How did the SDS agenda compare to President Johnson's? How did the Vietnam War affect the domestic agendas of both? Identify: Urban Renewal Act, Packinghouse Workers Union, Tom Hayden, Port Huron Statement.

VIETNAM: AMERICA'S LONGEST WAR: How long did the Vietnam conflict go on and how did the U.S. become involved before the Johnson administration? Why is 1964 considered the beginning for the U.S. in spite of previous involvement? What were the results of the war in terms of emotional and political fallout?

    Johnson's War: Why was the war referred to as Johnson's war? How did past history in China and Korea affect Johnson's decision? What was the Gulf of Tonkin resolution and what were the circumstances behind it? How did Johnson's advisors differ? Identify: Vietcong, Barry Goldwater.

    Deeper into the Quagmire: How did the U.S. become more and more involved in Vietnam? What were the changes in U.S. troop numbers from 1965 to 1966? What was the Johnson-Westmoreland strategy and on what did it depend? How heavily were the South and the North bombed in comparison to WWII? What were the differences of view between advisors and analysts over tactics? Identify: Operation Rolling Thunder.

    The Credibility Gap: What was the credibility gap and how did it develop? What was the role of the press during the Vietnam War? What changes occurred in press reactions? Who was J. William Fulbright and how did he add to the credibility gap? What happened in Congress within Johnson's own party? How did some of the European allies and the UN react? What was the impact of the war at home? Identify: Morley Safer, Eric Sevareid, Harrison Salisbury, Arrogance of Power.

A GENERATION IN CONFLICT: Why was the peace movement viewed as a generational conflict? Who were the baby boomers and flower children? How well educated was the sixties generation? How did the movement mobilize and spread?

    "The Times They are A-Changing:" How did the times change in this era? How did the free speech movement connect to civil rights? Who was Mario Savio and what views did he represent? What demands did students begin to make? What was the counterculture? What forms did generational rebellion take? What part did music play in defining the counterculture? To what extent did Woodstock represent young Americans? Identify: Haight-Ashbury, Timothy Leary, Beatles, folk music, Joan Baez, Bob Dylan, "Make Love, Not War," *The Greening of America.*

From Campus Protest to Mass Mobilization: How did the escalation of the war tie in to campus protest and its growth? Why did many students tie protest of the war to the university itself? What did students protest in addition to the war in Vietnam? How diverse did the peace movement eventually become? What opposition to the protesters developed? Identify: teach-in, Dow Chemical Company, Daniel and Philip Berrigan.

Teenage Soldiers: What was the average age of Vietnam soldiers compared to World War II soldiers? What split developed within the younger generation? What were the views of many young GIs? What happened to many when they came home? Identify: Selective Service Act, fragging, a white man's war.

WARS ON POVERTY: What prompted the new awareness of poverty? What were the arguments of Michael Harrington's *Other America?* What was Johnson's view of this issue?

The Great Society: What were Johnson's plans to achieve his Great Society? What were the following programs and their outcomes: OEO, Job Corps, Youth Corps, VISTA, CAP, Legal Services Program, Community Health Centers, Upward Bound? What groups worked against the programs? Where did spending on social welfare actually go? Why didn't it affect the root of poverty?

Crisis in the Cities: What was the crisis in the city? What were the causes? How did many government programs make the crisis worse? What population migrations continued to come to cities? Identify: white flight, redlining, Negro removal.

Urban Uprisings: What was the extent of urban uprisings from 1964 to 1968? What were the reasons for the uprisings? How were these riots different from earlier race riots? What was the significance of Watts, Newark and Detroit? What was the Kerner Commission and its findings? What happened to the Commission's recommendations? What was Fulbright's critique?

1968: What is the significance of 1968 as a turning point for American foreign and domestic politics? What major violence developed?

The Tet Offensive: What was the Tet Offensive and what effects did it have in Vietnam and domestically? What was Johnson's response?

King, the War, and the Assassination: How did Martin Luther King, Jr. shift his position by 1965? What happened to some of his support? Why was he in Memphis when he was assassinated? What types of reactions developed to his assassination? What happened to the vision of "Beloved Community?"

The Democratic Campaign: What different candidates campaigned for the Democratic presidential nomination? What happened to Robert Kennedy just as he seemed unbeatable? Who won the nomination and why was he chosen? Identify: children's crusade.

The Whole World Is Watching: What event is being referred to here? Why was so much attention focused on the Democratic convention and what divisions could be seen? How had the protest become worldwide? Identify: Yippies, Abbie

Hoffman, Richard Daley, McCarthy headquarters, police riot, Abraham Ribicoff, "Be Realistic, Demand the Impossible."

THE POLITICS OF IDENTITY: What various groups searched for identity as the cultures of protest grew? What successes did they have? What similarities did they have to the earlier civil rights and antiwar groups? Identify: the Establishment.

Black Power: What was the major directional shift of the civil rights movement signified by Black Power? What shift did Stokely Carmichael make in SNCC? What were the key tenets of Black Power? What was the boldest expression of Black Power? How did Jesse Jackson work to enact Black Power in Operation Breadbasket? What was the most enduring component of Black Power and what changes were demanded? Identify: Black Panthers, Huey Newton and Bobby Seale, Black Power, Muhammed Ali, Kwanzaa, Black is Beautiful.

Sisterhood Is Powerful: What various writings, reports and attitudes helped spur political awareness among women? How did part of this result form unequal treatment in the earlier protest groups? What class and ethnic differences were there in the women's liberation movement? Identify: National Organization for Women, consciousness-raising groups, Kate Millet's *Sexual Politics.*

Gay Liberation: What various groups had fought for gay liberation before the 1960s and how did it expand in the 1960s? What was the Stonewall Riot and its significance? What was the GLF and what tactics did it adopt from the civil rights and antiwar movements? What changes in public opinion and policies were gained?

The Chicano Rebellion: What was the significance of the term *Chicano?* What actions did the Chicano movement take? What regional movements were inspired by Chicano nationalism? What did many activists discover? Identify: *la raza,* Bilingual Education Act, Brown Berets, *Chicanismo,* Corky Gonzale's Crusade for justice.

Red Power: How did Indian pride reassert itself and what events demonstrated it? What was the American Indian Movement and what were its goals? What were its failures and victories? What was the Indian Renaissance and what were its major works? Identify: George Mitchell, Dennis Banks, Native American Rights Fund.

The Asian American Movement: What degree of activism was there in the various Asian American communities? What commonality was there with the Black and Latino movements? What did they encourage in educational curriculums? What were the limits of the politics of identity? Identify: Gooks, *Woman Warrior, Sansei.*

THE NIXON PRESIDENCY: What did Nixon base his presidency on in terms of conservatism? Who was the silent majority according to Republican strategists? What major foreign policy moves did Nixon make? To what extent did he satisfy his constituency?

The Southern Strategy: What area of the country did Republican leaders recognize in their campaign and why did they follow this strategy? Who did Nixon choose for his running mate? What was the basis of Wallace's third party candidacy?

Nixon's War: How did the Vietnam War become Nixon's war instead of Johnson's? Who was responsible for prolonging the conflict? What "knockout blow" did Nixon decide to carry out and how did many people react? What happened at Kent State and Jackson State Universities? What was the Paris Peace Agreement of January 1973? Identify: Henry Kissinger, "Vietnamization," William L. Calley.

The China Card: What was the China Card and why did Nixon play it? How could he do this without affecting his popularity with conservatives? What was the Nixon Doctrine? What was the result for U.S. policy positions with the Soviet Union and with the Nationalist Chinese government? Identify: Ping pong diplomacy, SALT, shuttle diplomacy.

Domestic Policy: What were the basic elements of Nixon's domestic policy and the programs and legislation he sponsored? In what areas did Nixon become more liberal and in what areas did he stay conservative? Identify: Environmental Protection Agency, Occupational Safety and Health Administration, black capitalism, Warren Burger, *Apollo 11*.

WATERGATE: What situations led to Watergate? What was the extent of Watergate? What events surrounding Watergate finally led to President Nixon's resignation?

Foreign Policy as Conspiracy: What was foreign policy as conspiracy and how was it being challenged by 1970? How did Nixon respond? What were the various covert programs being carried on during Nixon's administration? How did these become known? Identify: Anastazio Somoza, Salvador Allende.

The Age of Dirty Tricks: What were the "dirty tricks" and who was playing them? Who were the "plumbers" and why was Daniel Ellsberg their first target? What was their most ambitious trick and what happened as a result? Why did televised hearings make the situation even more dramatic? Identify: E. Howard Hunt, G. Gordon Liddy, George McGovern, CREEP, Saturday Night Massacre.

The Fall of the Executive: How did the case against Nixon solidify and force his resignation? What was the Agnew debacle? Who did Nixon choose to replace Agnew?

CONCLUSION: What were the results of the Nixon and Agnew resignations for the national mood? What type of legacy did Watergate leave? Identify: War Powers Act.

CHRONOLOGY: Apply the standard questions from p. 4 of the Study Guide.

STUDY SKILLS EXERCISES

1. Reflections: If you had been on a college campus in 1965, how do you think you might have reacted to the escalation of the war? How would you have reacted if you were drafted? What type of reaction, mood, feelings might you have had by the end of the events of 1968? How might you have reacted if you were not on a campus?

2. Making connections: chapters 27 and 28: Consider how the critics of mass culture like Paul Goodman and the Beat writers anticipated the counter culture and youth movement of the 1960s and how the energy of the civil rights movement added to it as well. Music continued to provide identity. Discuss how the war gave it more energy and yet diverted the goals of groups like the SDS in a search for meaningful community. Compare the black activist views of Martin Luther King to those of Stokely Carmichael and Malcolm X. Consider the connection between Eisenhower's and Mill's warning of a military-industrial complex and student actions.

3. Vocabulary:

mobilize, p. 879	turbulent, p. 892
subversion, p. 881	redlined, p. 894
resonated, p. 884	tenets, p. 897
inducements, p. 887	discord, p. 903
exodus, p. 890	surreptitious, p. 907

4. Maps:
   a. *Anti-War Protests on College and University Campuses, 1967-1969:* (p. 886) Where were campus-based protests centered in the United States when they first began? Where did they spread? Where were most protests centered in western Europe?
   b. *Urban Uprisings, 1965-1968:* (p. 891) What did rioters take aim at in their communities? In general, where were most urban uprisings? What states and cities experienced the most uprisings?
   c. *Major Indian Reservations, 1976:* (p. 900) Generally, where were most Indian reservations located in 1976? What states east of the Mississippi had reservations? Which of the eastern states had the largest number? Compare this map to the one on p. 548 in chapter 18. Which state(s) had increased areas of reservation in 1976 compared to the earlier map?
   d. *The Southeast Asian* War: (p. 893) Be able to locate South and North Vietnam and Cambodia. Locate the following: Gulf of Tonkin, Saigon, Hanoi.
   e. *Election of 1968:* (p. 903) What area was generally won by George Wallace? What area that was traditionally Democratic from FDR days was lost by Democrats in 1968?

RECITE/REVIEW

MULTIPLE CHOICE:

1. The carrying out of the Urban Renewal Act in the community of Uptown meant that the
   a. housing would be upgraded for middle-class families.
   b. government would help end poverty in the neighborhood.
   c. city would have civilian review boards to curb police harassment.
   d. citizens would be federally empowered to change their lives.

2. Part of Johnson's motivation in being involved in Vietnam is that he did not want Vietnam to be to him as this was to Truman:
   a. China and Korea
   b. Eastern Europe
   c. Greece and Turkey
   d. Philippines

3. The Free Speech Movement at the University of California in 1964 was created when university administrators tried to prevent students from
   a. protesting the escalation of the war in Vietnam.
   b. protesting segregation and other civil rights issues.
   c. joining the United Farm Workers in a strike.
   d. holding "teach-ins" and "be-ins."

4. The "teach-in" united these two movements:
   a. student free speech and protesting the war
   b. civil rights and student demonstrations
   c. SNCC and La Raza
   d. Nation of Islam and Black Panthers

5. One of the centerpieces of President Johnson's War on Poverty was the OEO, or Office of_____Opportunity:
   a. Equal
   b. Economic
   c. Educational
   d. Employment

6. The first major urban riot of 1964-1968 took place in the Watts section of
   a. Newark, New Jersey.
   b. Los Angeles, California.
   c. San Francisco, California.
   d. Detroit, Michigan.

7. The Kerner Commission concluded that the basic cause of the widespread racial violence of the mid-1960s was
   a. criminal lawlessness.
   b. campus radical agitation.
   c. the Vietnam War and unequal rights.
   d. white racism.

8. Which one of the following is NOT correctly matched to the group it represents?
   a. SDS: Students for a Democratic Society
   b. GLF: Gay Liberation Front
   c. AIM: Asian Independence Movement
   d. NOW: National Organization for Women

9. The great increase in war protests nationwide with the tragedies at Kent State and Jackson State came about from this policy decision:
   a. Operation Rolling Thunder
   b. My Lai search-and-destroy
   c. the Tet Offensive
   d. the bombing of Cambodia

10. "Ping-pong diplomacy" symbolized the dramatic changes Nixon made in U.S. policy toward
    a. North Vietnam.
    b. the Soviet Union.
    c. the Peoples Republic of China.
    d. the Middle East crisis.

11. SALT was a major breakthrough treaty between the United States and the Soviet Union, with the "A" signifying its core of the agreement. The "A" refers to
    a. Air space.
    b. Arms.
    c. Asian.
    d. Atlantic.

12. Which one of the following is NOT a regime that Nixon sent arms to during his administration?
    a. Shah of Iran
    b. Botha of South Africa
    c. Marcos of Philippines
    d. Allende of Chile

CHRONOLOGY AND MAPS:

13. Which answer gives the correct order of the following:
    (1) the Pentagon papers were published.
    (2) Vietnam Veterans Against the War was formed.
    (3) the Watergate break-in occurred.
    (4) Vietnam peace talks begin in Paris.
        a. 2,4,1,3
        b. 3,2,4,1
        c. 4,1,2,3
        d. 1,3,2,4

14. Which one of the following does NOT happen in 1964?
    a. Johnson declares a war on poverty.
    b. Gulf of Tonkin resolution.
    c. Watts uprising.
    d. Free speech movement begins at Berkeley.

15. 1969 marks the hightide of the counterculture
    a. at University of California at Berkeley.
    b. in the "Summer of Love."
    c. with the Sheep's Meadow antiwar rally.
    d. at the Woodstock music festival.

16. Most early campus-based protests were in
    a. California and on the East Coast.
    b. Europe and then spread to the U.S.
    c. the South and Midwest.
    d. the West and Great Plains.

17. These two states had an increase in the area added to Indian reservations by 1976:
    a. New Mexico and Arizona
    b. Oregon and Nevada
    c. Kansas and Oklahoma
    d. North and South Dakota

SHORT ESSAY:

    18. What led to the urban uprisings of the 1960s?

    19. What were the goals of the Black Power movement?

    20. What led to Nixon's victory in the 1968 presidential election?

EXTENDED ESSAY:

    21. Analyze the role of television in influencing Americans' reactions to the war in Vietnam.

    22. What factors led to U.S. defeat in Vietnam?

    23. Evaluate Nixon's foreign policy successes and failures.

ANSWERS-CHAPTER 29

MULTIPLE CHOICE:

1.	a, pp. 879-80	7.	d, p. 892
2.	a, p. 881	8.	c, p. 901
3.	b, p. 884	9.	d, p. 904
4.	a, p. 886	10.	c, p. 906
5.	b, p. 888	11.	b, p. 906
6.	b, p. 892	12.	b, p. 907

CHRONOLOGY AND MAPS:

13.	a, p. 909	16.	a, p. 886
14.	c, p. 909	17.	a, p. 900
15.	d, p. 909		

SHORT ESSAY:
18-20

EXTENDED ESSAY:
21-23

30

THE OVER-EXTENDED SOCIETY, 1974—1980

SURVEY

Chapter Overview: This chapter covers the Ford and Carter administrations and their attempts to respond to national emergencies with a "lick your plate clean" and take personal responsibility approach which did not go over well with the public. Americans discovered the high price of defense in the Cold War but in the aftermath of Watergate had little confidence in the federal government. Grass roots political activity increased but did not expand nationally. A new conservatism driven by a revived religious right was energetic but failed to solve the nation's malaise. America's industrial base would continue to erode. Both the Soviets and Americans would come to realize they could not continue The Cold War. Western Europe, Latin America and Japan increased their share of the world market while the U.S. floundered with its energy problems, persistent poverty and environmental issues.

Chapter Objectives: After reading this chapter and following the study suggestions given. you should be able to:

1. Summarize the issues involved in the Three Mile Island, Pennsylvania nuclear problem.
2. Explain stagflation, the problems that perpetuated it and federal government response during the administrations of Ford and Carter.
3. Discuss the basis of the new poverty of the 1970s.
4. Summarize the activities of grass roots politics and the politics of the new.
5. Outline the various foreign policy problems of the Ford and Carter administrations and how they responded to them.
6. Analyze how all of the above items led to the Republican victory in the 1980 election.
7. Making Connections: How did many of the foreign policy issues Carter dealt with illustrate the consequences of policies dating from the 1870s?

QUESTIONS/READ

AMERICAN COMMUNITIES: Three Mile Island, Pennsylvania: What was the near disaster at Three Mile Island, Pennsylvania and how did the community respond to it? What were NIMBYS and how did they work to prevent another TMI? When did the promotion of nuclear energy begin and what effect did the near-disaster at TMI have on it? How was this symbolic of the chapter title, "The Overextended Society?"

STAGFLATION: What was stagflation and what were the statistics of it in economic growth, unemployment and inflation? How was the U.S. world standing affected? According to polls at the end of the 1970s, what did Americans believe about the future? What were the main economic problems?

The Oil Crisis: What was OPEC and how did it precipitate an energy crisis? How did the potential for the crisis already exist since the 1950s? How did Americans respond to the Arabs and to the oil companies?

The Bill Comes Due: What conservation measures did President Nixon invoke? What effect did the energy prices have on other prices and how was this different from the previous century? What group's lifestyle was affected? Identify: energy czar, Department of Energy.

Falling Productivity: What happened to American productivity in the steel industry compared to Western Europe, Latin America and Japan? What were some of the deeper causes of decline? What amount of steel did America produce in 1975 compared to 1947? What other industries were affected? How did major American corporations respond? What was the grim picture in agriculture? Identify: Lordstown, Ohio, outsourced, Quality work life circles.

Blue-Collar Blues: What were the causes of the blue-collar blues? What change had occurred in the National Labor Relations Board rulings? What area of the work force did grow in organized labor in this era? How many women were in the work force and what was their experience in wage averages from 1955 to 1980? What gains did African American women make: Latinos? What effect did groups like Nine to Five have? How did the AFL-CIO respond?

Sunbelt/Snowbelt: What were the sunbelt and snowbelt and what was happening in each in terms of the economy? Why were more people moving to sunbelt areas? What were America's three most populous states? What was the down side of the sunbelt? Identify: golden age migration, black migration, Silicon Valley, Rustbelt.

"LEAN YEARS" PRESIDENTS: Who were the lean years presidents and how did they attempt to deal with the decline? What happened to voter participation and why?

"I'm a Ford, Not a Lincoln:" What was the implication of Gerald Ford's comment that he was a Ford and not a Lincoln? What problems did Ford face as president and what was his program to rejuvenate the economy? How did Ford respond to emergency bills passed by Congress? How did people respond to First Lady Betty Ford by comparison to the president? Identify: WIN.

The 1976 Election: Who were the candidates in the election of 1976 and what were the issues in the election? Why were the Republicans reluctant to nominate

Reagan? What was the proposed program of Carter? How well did each candidate run in various parts of the country and how well did the voters turn out?

The Carter Presidency: What problems did Carter run into with the economy and with his own style during his presidency? What was Carter's sense of political reality? Why was Carter not likely to reinvoke New Deal or Great Society initiatives? What economic elements were Carter's worst domestic enemies? Identify: superfund.

THE NEW POVERTY: What was different about the poverty of the mid-1970s? What was Michael Harrington's evaluation of it?

A Two-Tiered Society: What were the two tiers of society in the 1970s and how did that connect to the new poverty? What were the statistics of poverty including the gap race? What differences occurred among black Americans and what were sociologist William Julius Wilson's observations about it? What did other scholars have to say? What was Boston symbolic of in relation to integration of schools? What was the Bakke decision about affirmative action?

Feminization of Poverty: What is the meaning of feminization of poverty and what are the statistics of it? How did the average standard of living of divorced men compare to that of divorced women? What were these trends like in the African American and Puerto Rican communities? What reinforced this pattern in the black community? What were the findings of sociologist Diana Pearce?

A Permanent Underclass: What was the permanent underclass Senator Kennedy referred to? Why was the word permanent used? What were the statistics of the underclass? Which states and/or areas had the poorest people? How did sociologists connect poverty to the rising crime rate? How were Indians affected and what were the statistics of poverty for them? What were the decisions of *United States v. Wheeler* and *Oliphant v. Squamish Indian Tribe?*

COMMUNITIES AND GRASS-ROOTS POLITICS: How and why did political activism shift to the community levels? What types of issues were the center of attention? What were the overall effects of these activities?

The New Urban Politics: What was the success of urban coalitions and how successful were various minority groups? What was the meaning of Maynard Johnson's comment about civil rights and politics? What was the significance of Mississippi in minority political success? How did minorities improve their position and how did the fiscal crises of the 1970s limit their gains?

The City and the Neighborhood: What efforts were made to save cities and neighborhoods from decline? What was the goal of President Carter's National Commission on Neighborhoods and how was this stifled or diverted? Identify: Community Development Act of 1914, COPS, ACORN, Community Development Corporations, Community Boards, gentrification.

The Endangered Environment: To what extent was the environment endangered and how did grass roots politics connect to it? What were the points of Frances Moore Lappe's and Barry Commoner's works? What successes and defeats did the environmentalists experience? Identify: Love Canal, *Silent Spring,* Audubon

Society, Wilderness Society, Sierra Club, Greenpeace, Environmental Protection Agency, Alaska Pipeline.

Small-Town America: What trends characterized small-town America? What was the low density "exurbia" trend? Why didn't this growth rejuvenate small town centers and local merchants? What was the 1974 grass roots campaign in Vermont symbolic of? What small towns declined and what was the "snowball effect" that they experienced? Identify: *Small is Beautiful.*

THE NEW CONSERVATISM: What was the new conservatism and what groups made up the growth of conservative voters? What was the symbolism of Proposition 13 in California? How did this affect politics?

The New Right: What groups made up the New Right or neo conservatives? What religious groups and new religious organizations gave the New Right a greater boost? Besides communists, who was added to the list of "enemies" by leaders like Jerry Falwell? Who was Jesse Helms and how did he make use of the New Right politically? Identify: *Turner Diaries,* Moral 'Majority, direct mail, televangelists.

Anti-ERA, Anti-abortion: Why did the New Right particularly concentrate on the two issues of the ERA and abortion policies? Who was Phyllis Schlafly and her STOP ERA campaign? What was the *Roe v. Wade* decision and what campaign took shape as a result? Identify: ERA, Hyde Amendment.

The "Me Decade:" Who coined the term "me decade" and what did it mean? What observations did historian Christopher Lasch make in this work *The Culture of Narcissism?* What was the human potential movement and what were some of the groups that became popular? What religious cults of the right and left developed? How did popular music reflect changes of the late 1960s and 1970s?

ADJUSTING TO A NEW WORLD: What adjustments did Americans make in foreign policy? What was the new realism of Ford and Carter? Identify: "NO More Vietnams."

A Thaw in the Cold War: Why did a thaw develop in the Cold War for both the United States and the Soviet Union? What was the toll military spending exacted from the U.S. economy? What was the Helsinki conference agreement? Why did SALT II fail to win confirmation from the Senate? What was Walter Lippman's observation?

Foreign Policy and "Moral Principles:" What connection between morality and foreign policy did President Carter make? How consistent was he? What was the legacy of a century that affected most of Carter's decisions? What nations were criticized in terms of human rights and which ones were not? What group did Carter try to clean up and what happened to his efforts? What changes were embodied in the Panama Canal treaties?

The Camp David Accords: What success did Carter achieve in the Camp David Accords? What were the terms of the agreement? Why didn't this achievement extend to the rest of the Middle East? Identify: Menachem Begin, Anwar el-Sadat.

CARTER'S CRISIS OF CONFIDENCE: What was Carter's "crisis of confidence" speech and how did the public and the press respond? What might have helped Carter restore his standing and what happened instead?

(Mis) Handling the Unexpected: What series of unexpected crises in foreign policy occurred and how was each handled? What feud between Cyrus Vance, Secretary of State, and Zbigniew Brzezinski, National Security Advisor, made the situations worse? What happened to the Cold War under President Carter? Identify: Anastasio Somoza, Andrew Young, Nigeria and Angola, Afghanistan, Carter Doctrine, Presidential Directive 59.

The Iran Hostage Crisis: How did the Iran hostage crisis occur? What policy did the U.S. have in Iran and how did Carter continue it? What advice did Carter follow and what happened? What was the political and economic fallout? Identify: Ayatollah Ruholla Khomeini, Mohammed Reza Pahlavi, Great Satan.

The 1980 Election: What prospects did Carter have for re-election? What other surprise developed in foreign policy? What unified opposition did Carter face from Republicans? What were the results of the election? What was the voter turnout? Identify: Marielitos, Conservative Revolution.

CONCLUSION: What debacle and what hopeful signs marked the end of the Nixon, Ford and Carter years? What continued to make U.S. economic problems worse?

CHRONOLOGY: Apply the standard questions from p. 4 of the Study Guide.

STUDY SKILLS EXERCISES

1. Reflections:
   a. How would you have voted (or how did you vote) and why in the 1976 and 1980 elections?
   b. Should Carter have paid more attention to Cyrus Vance's or Zbigniew Brzezinski's advice in foreign policy?
   c. How significant is grass roots politics to you as a way to solve problems?
   d. Was the "me decade" new or were we returning to an earlier era after a period of high involvement and expectation? Do you agree with Tom Wolfe or Christopher Lasch in the first place? Why or why not?
   e. Do you think the title of this chapter, "The Over Extended Society" is accurate? What title would you give it?

2. Making connections:
   a. Chapter 22: Your text states that Vance was the first secretary of state in 65 years to resign over principle. Who was the previous one?
   b. Chapter 22: How well do you think Presidents Carter and Wilson would have coincided on foreign policy principle? Do you find any irony in both of them having secretaries of state resigning?
   c. Chapter 28: Compare the new poverty to the poverty issues discussed in the Great Society.
   d. Chapter 17: Compare the decline of the civil rights movement to the decline after Reconstruction.
   e. Chapter 19: Compare the South's share of sunbelt success to the idea of the New South. Would Henry Woodfin Grady approve?

3. Vocabulary:
   meltdown, p. 914   disparity, p. 925
   cartel, p. 916   touchstone, p. 928
   bounty, p. 918   evangelical, p. 932
   agribusiness, p. 921   cults, p. 934
   apathy, p. 923   coups, p. 939

4. Maps:
   a. *1970s: Oil Consumption:* (pp. 918-919) What does OPEC mean and what countries are part of it? What happened to the price of oil and energy prices in the 1970s? What happened in the economy? What does stagflation mean? What two unanticipated consequences happened?
   b. *Population Shifts, 1970-1980:* (p. 922) What overall shifts occurred in the population? What two events coincided to cause this? What states gained 20% or more in population? What states had a loss or only a small gain? In what general area(s) were the states that had a 10-19.9% gain? What northern state is in that category?
   c. *Election of 1976:* (p. 923) What areas of the country did Carter carry? Which sections did Ford carry?

RECITE/REVIEW

MULTIPLE CHOICE:

1. The events at Three Mile Island reinforced a wave of
   a. community-based mobilizations against nuclear power.
   b. construction of new nuclear plants in the far West.
   c. desire to be free of foreign energy sources.
   d. stagflation.

2. Which one of the following is NOT an example of the economic problems of the United States in the early to mid-1970s?
   a. U.S. standard of living dropped to fifth in world rankings
   b. U.S. dependence on foreign oil grew to 36 percent
   c. U.S. steel production dropped from 60 to 17 percent.
   d. U.S. Silicon Valley lost production edge to Japan.

3. Critics called Carter a Democrat who talked and thought like a Republican. Which one of the following was NOT one of his actions that seemed to reinforce that?
   a. He sought to reduce the scale of federal government.
   b. He deregulated airlines and banks from federal control.
   c. He created a superfund to clean up abandoned toxic waste sites.
   d. He did not feel redistributing power and wealth would help problems.

4. While the Sunbelt states experienced growth, this state was still among those that accounted for the largest pockets of poverty nationwide:
   a. Texas
   b. New Mexico
   c. Florida
   d. Mississippi

5. Frances Moore Lappe and Barry Commoner both argued that people had to accept the
   a. "politics of the possible."
   b. restoration of "traditional family values."
   c. balance and limits of "small is beautiful."
   d. fact that the U.S. could not run and police the whole world.

6. Which one of the following was NOT an example of the new conservatism?
   a. passage of Proposition 13 in California
   b. decrease in voter participation among conservatives
   c. popularity of the Moral Majority
   d. Phyllis Schafly's STOP ERA

7. The first major politician to realize the power of the New Right and appeal directly to it for fundraising was
   a. Ronald Reagan.
   b. Jerry Ford.
   c. Jesse Helms.
   d. George Bush.

8. In terms of conservatism, which one of the following has the LEAST in common with the other three?
   a. Sun Myung Moon
   b. Jim Jones
   c. Pat Robertson
   d. Jerry Falwell

9. The 1975 conference in Helsinki, Finland moved away from the Cold War days by
   a. establishing a second SALT treaty.
   b. accepting the boundaries of countries drawn after World War II.
   c. having all major powers agree to stay neutral in the Arab-Israeli conflict.
   d. limiting world arms sales.

10. Which one of these areas came out successfully for Carter in terms of his policies?
    a. Iran
    b. Panama
    c. Nicaragua
    d. Cuba

11. Which one of the following was NOT a part of the Camp David Accords?
    a. Egypt recognized the existence of Israel as a state.
    b. Israel gave the Sinai Peninsula back to Egypt.
    c. Egypt agreed to supply oil to the United States.
    d. The "legitimate rights of the Palestinians" were vaguely agreed to.

12. Soviet invasion of Afghanistan prompted critics to call it the "Russian Vietnam" because of this similarity:
    a. they got caught in an unwinnable civil war with guerrillas against them.
    b. they fabricated a pretext for moving in there in the first place.
    c. they were trying to counter U.S. influence in Afghanistan.
    d. major protests broke out in the Soviet Union.

13. The commonality between Cyrus Vance and William Jennings Bryan resigning as secretary of state was that they both
    a. advocated negotiation instead of any seemingly belligerent action.
    b. believed in staying out of the issue in the first place.
    c. were in favor of the League/United Nations dealing with the problems.
    d. were compromised by scandalous involvement in clandestine activities.

14. Which one of the following Supreme Court cases is NOT correctly matched with the decision?
    a. *Bakke/* affirmative action could operate only when a legacy of unequal treatment could be proven.
    b. *Roe v. Wade/*state laws prohibiting abortions in the first two trimesters constituted a violation of a woman's right of privacy.
    c. *Oliphant v. Squamish Indian Tribe/*tribes could not arrest or punish trespassers who violated their laws.
    d. *United States v. Wheeler/*National Labor Relations Board had to take management needs into account.

CHRONOLOGY AND MAPS:

15. Which one of the following did NOT occur in 1978?
    a. *Bakke v. University of California* decision
    b. Panama Canal treaties
    c. Middle East peace accord at Camp David
    d. Three Mile Island nuclear accident

16. The only northern state to experience a high gain of population in the 1970s was
    a. Vermont.
    c. New Hampshire.
    b. New York.
    d. Iowa.

SHORT ESSAY:

17. What factors contributed to the economic problems of the 1970s?

18. What problems plagued the Ford Administration?

19. What contributed to the widening gap between the rich and the poor in the 1970s?

EXTENDED ESSAY:

20. Analyze the emergence of American conservatism in the late 1970s.

21. Analyze Jimmy Carter's foreign policy strengths and weaknesses.

22. In retrospect, was the Republican Party's decision to reject Ronald Reagan as its candidate in 1976 a poor one? Defend your answer.

ANSWERS-CHAPTER 30

MULTIPLE CHOICE:
1. a, p. 914
2. d, p 921
3. c, p. 924
4. a, p. 928
5. a, p. 929-30
6. b, p. 931-4
7. c, p. 932
8. b, p. 932
9. b, p. 936
10. b, p. 936
11. c, p. 937-8
12. a, p. 939
13. a, p. 940
14. d, p. 927

CHRONOLOGY AND MAPS:
15. d, p. 941
16. c, p. 922

SHORT ESSAY:
17-19

EXTENDED ESSAY: 20-22

31

THE CONSERVATIVE ASCENDANCY, 1980—1992

SURVEY

Chapter Overview: This chapter covers the shift of the American economy from manufacturing and industry to a service and information based economy. Another shift was noted in the 1990 census. For the first time, the majority of Americans lived in a metropolitan area. A third shift was the end of the Cold War. Americans struggled to adjust to these changes, looking first to the Reagan-Bush presidencies for answers. Reagan's own personal shift from a New Deal Democrat to a Republican that rejected activist welfare but still admired FDR's inspiring leadership perhaps paralleled a shift among many American voters. Democrats under Clinton recaptured the presidency by being more centrist themselves, but they were continually challenged by a resurgent Right. Economic competition with Europe and Pacific Rim nations would replace the Cold War ideological struggles but problems would still remain in various areas including the Middle East. Presidents Bush and Clinton would look for more collective actions through the U.N. than the U.S. alone. Economic shifts to service industry and less need for the military industrial complex continued to reinforce the growing inequities among Americans. American communities struggled to respond to a more global, service-oriented, high tech economy with the potential of various regional solutions as they faced the 21st century.

Chapter Objectives: After reading this chapter and following the study suggestions given, you should be able to

1. describe the different versions of community on the electronic frontier of cyberspace.
2. explain the successes and limitations of the Reagan Revolution through the Reagan and Bush administrations.
3. summarize the dramatic socio-economic changes in America including a shift to a service-based and high tech information economy, a more electronic culture and a more metropolitan society.
4. discuss the problems that accompanied the changes listed in the overview, including the epidemics of drugs, AIDS and homelessness and the multicultural riot in Los Angeles.
5. trace the policy of President Reagan and the evil empire as well as the changes and continuing issues under Reagan and Bush.
6. discuss the issues of the 1992 presidential campaign as they relate to the above trends.
7. describe the "American renewal" of Clinton and the resurgence of the right under Gingrich.

AMERICAN COMMUNITIES: **Virtual communities on the electronic frontier:** What are virtual communities? What was ARPANET and what unexpected grass roots connections resulted? What are both the democratic and exploitative possibilities of virtual communities? What are WELL and Prodigy and what are the differences between them? Identify: hackers, Internet, WELL, Prodigy, Communication Decency Act.

THE REAGAN REVOLUTION: What was the Reagan Revolution and to what extent did it succeed?

The Great Communicator: Why was President Reagan called the great communicator? What was his occupational and political background before he became president? Why was Reagan more successful in being nominated in 1980 than in 1976 or 1968?

Reaganomics: What type of economic beliefs made up Reaganomics? Who was George Gilder and what were his economic views? What legislation was based on these ideas? What happened to deregulation? What officials in what areas carried out deregulation? What various results were there with deregulation?

Military Buildup: What were Reagan's views on a strong military? How did he build on Carter's defense spending? What was SDI and how did Reagan view it? How did the military industrial complex increase in the 1980s and how was it a shift in priority?

Recession, Recovery, Fiscal Crisis: What was the cycle of recession, recovery and fiscal crisis? What were the statistics of each stage? What were the different views on why these changes were occurring? While there was a deficit before, what structural problem with it occurred in the Reagan years? Why did this happen?

The Election of 1984: What issues were significant in the election of 1984? What was the "cultural democrat" or Hollywood persona Reagan embodied? How effectively did he win the 1984 election?

REAGAN'S FOREIGN POLICY: What were the basic principles of Reagan's foreign policy? What happened overall to the Cold War framework of American foreign policy?

The Evil Empire: What was the evil empire and how did Reagan propose to deal with it? What did the Reagan administration argue and critics dispute? Why did the Reagan advisors view of nuclear war bother some critics? What happened to any meaningful arms control in this atmosphere?

Central America: Why did Central America become a concern for American foreign policy? How did it fit with Reagan's views? What was the Reagan Doctrine or declaration? What was the Caribbean Basin Initiative and what happened to it? How did Latin Americans react to CBI? How much did spending increase? What developed in Grenada, El Salvador and Nicaragua and what was the U.S. response in each case? Identify: Sandinistas, Somoza, Contras, Boland Amendment, Iran-Contra Affair.

Glasnost and Arms Control: What was *glasnost* and what effect did it have on arms control negotiations between the United States and the Soviet Union? What were the historical ironies of the Gorbachev changes? Identify: *perestroika,* zero option, INF Treaty.

The Iran-Contra Scandal: What was the Iran-Contra scandal? How did *glasnost* affect it? What Middle East events did the U.S. become involved in? Who did the Reagan administration insist was behind the problems? How was the function of the National

Security Council changed to evade Congress? Identify: William Casey, John Poindexter, Oliver North, Tower Report.

BEST OF TIMES, WORST OF TIMES: What were the successes and limitations of America's economic and social changes during the 1980s? How was the notion of community changed?

Silicon Valley: Where was Silicon Valley and why was it significant? Why was it called Silicon Valley and how had it developed and flourished? What type of culture did it represent? How evenly was economic success enjoyed by various groups? What happened to the boom of Silicon Valley and where did many companies go? What other competition developed? Identify: Steve Jobs, Nolan Bushnell.

Monongahela Valley: What economic transformation took place in the Monongahela Valley? What were the causes of its decline by the 1980s? What was the policy of disinvestment and how did it hurt the area? What happened to overall employment? What happened to Clairton as an example of these changes?

Indian Country: What types of changes developed among Indian communities? How did self-determination affect the lives of most Indians? Where do many Indians live? What happened during the Reagan administration? What were the economies of many reservations like? How did that lead to opening casinos? What is Foxwood and how successful has it been? What negative things have occurred? Identify: *United States v. John,* Indian Gaming Regulatory Act of 1988, Mashantucket Pequots.

An Electronic Culture: What was the basis of an electronic culture and how did these technologies affect culture? What is compunications and the postindustrial society? What changes occurred in television technology and programming? What were the dominant themes of popular culture? How did demographic analysis affect community? Identify: yuppies, plutography.

Epidemics: Drugs, AIDS, Homelessness: What were the statistics of the epidemics of drugs, AIDS, and the homeless? Why were they more of a problem than before? What groups made up the homeless population? Identify: war on drugs, C. Everett Koop, ACT-UP.

Economic Woes: What were the major economic woes and how did the government try to respond? What is the Balanced Budget and Emergency Deficit Control Act? How did it mask the true size of the deficit? What was the difference between the Wall Street Crash of the 1980s and that of the 1920s? Identify: Ivan Boesky, Michael Millken, paper entrepreneurialism?

Growing Inequality: What were the dimensions of growing inequality? What two cherished assumptions of Americans were challenged during this time? How did family income compare? What happened to average weekly earnings for American workers? Why did many new jobs not really help increase weekly earnings? What happened in the growth of poverty?

END OF AN ERA: How did the end of the Cold War era change the American nation's foreign policy premises? What were the changes that ended the era?

The Election of 1988: What were the issues in the 1988 election? Who were the candidates for both parties and what were their backgrounds? What did the 1988 election signify in terms of the media? Identify: Lee Atwater, Willie Horton.

The New Immigration: Who were the new immigrants and how numerous were they? What states received most of the newcomers? How had the Immigration Reform Act of 1965 affected this change? What was the content of the Immigration Reform and Control Act of 1987?

The Collapse of Communism: What eventually happened to the Soviet state under Gorbachev? What other areas of communism collapsed as well? What was the significance of the Berlin Wall? Why was Gorbachev not able to succeed in changing the economy? Identify: solidarity, Yeltsin, Commonwealth of Independent States.

The Persian Gulf War: How did the U.S. become involved in a war in the Persian Gulf? Why did Iraq invade Kuwait and why did Americans respond with Operation Desert Shield? What shift developed to a more offensive position and eventually Operation Desert Storm? How did most Americans respond to Desert Storm? How was the press controlled? What questions remained unanswered and problems unsolved? Identify: Saddam Hussein, Kuwait, Norman Schwarzkopf, Colin Powell.

Multicultural Riot in Los Angeles: What were the causes, immediate and structural, of the riot in Los Angeles? What was the multicultural aspect of it? How did it compare to the Watts riot of 1965? How did the African American situation in Los Angeles reflect trends of the 1980s?

The Election of 1992: What were the issues and who were the candidates in the 1992 election? What was the fundamental international issue facing the country? How much had conservatives cut government spending? What was the clearest success for Reagan and Bush? What effect did Buchanan's primary challenge have on Bush? What did Buchanan and Pat Robertson try to do at the Republican convention? What was Clinton's background? What was the Perot wild card? How was the importance of the media demonstrated in this campaign? What group did Clinton concentrate on appealing to? How effectively did the Democrats win and where did Clinton run the best? What gains did women make in the election?

The Clinton Presidency and the Resurgent Right: What have been the goals of the Clinton presidency? What is the "new Democrat" stance? What successes and failures has President Clinton had? What problems and opposition were there to the Clinton health care plan? What are NAFTA and GATT and how did they split the Democrats? What happened in the 1994 congressional elections? Who is Newt Gingrich and what does he represent? What conditions worked to the Republican advantage? Identify: Hillary Rodham Clinton, Proposition 187, Contract with America.

Changing American Communities: What did the 1990 census show about the population in metropolitan areas? How was metropolitan defined? What were the two largest areas and where were the most rapidly growing areas? How was this connected to the expansion of the service sector? In what way was Plano, Texas a sign of the future in the American community?

CONCLUSION: What changes has global competition brought? What changes have occurred and will continue to do so in American communities?

CHRONOLOGY: Apply the standard questions from p. 4 of the Study Guide.

STUDY SKILLS EXERCISES

1. Reflections:
   a. How would you have voted (or did you vote) in the 1984, 1988, 1992, and 1994 elections? What would have been the significant issues to you? If you were registered to vote and didn't, why not?
   b. Gorbachev said he was going to do something terrible to us--deprive us of an enemy. Who has become the enemy? Is it necessary to see things in that way? How does it affect unity on the one hand and create disunity on the other?
   c. What regional solutions do you see to American economic adjustments?
   d. Consider whether war is an appropriate metaphor for dealing with problems like drugs or diseases.

2. Making connections: Chapters 27 - 30:
   a. To what extent do you think Reagan's shift from a New Deal Democrat to a Republican parallels a shift of a significant number of American voters?
   b. Chapter 23: It was not uncommon for commentators to compare the U.S. of the 1980s to the U.S. of the 1920s. Analyze and evaluate the validity of such a comparison.
   c. Chapter 27: President Eisenhower warned Americans about the problems of a military industrial complex. To what extent do you think this warning continued to be valid?
   d. Chapter 29: Compare the role of the press and freedom of reporters on the battlefield in Vietnam and the Persian Gulf War.
   e. Chapter 30: Carter's critics said he often talked like a Democrat and thought like a Republican. To what extent did Clinton do this while campaigning?

3. Vocabulary:

cyberspace, p. 946	corrosive, p. 961
supply side, p. 949	scourge, p. 964
deficit, p. 952	underwriting, p. 967
paramilitary, p. 955	amnesty, p. 971
sordid, p. 957	resurgent, p. 980
entrepreneurship, p. 959	

4. Maps:
   a. *The Election of 1980:* (p. 949) What group of voters did Reagan attract? What was the extent of his victory and Carter's loss?
   b. *The United States in Central America, 1978-1990:* (p. 954) What happened to U.S. intervention in Central America under Reagan? What areas were the major areas of concentration? Be able to locate the major countries including island countries and Grenada. Compare this map to those on pages 647 and 836. What countries has the U.S. been consistently involved in?
   c. *The United States in the Middle East in the 1980s:* (p. 957) What were the various areas of U.S. involvement in the 1980s? Be able to identify the countries of the Middle East as well as the following: Sinai Peninsula, West Bank, Gaza Strip, Golan Heights, Beirut, Baghdad, Basra, Teheran, Persian Gulf, Strait of Hormuz, Suez Canal.
   d. *Continent of Birth for Immigrants, 1981-1989:* (p. 970) Where did most immigrants to the U.S. come from in the 1980s; or the least?

RECITE/REVIEW

MULTIPLE CHOICE:

1. This 1985 community linked virtually by computer and in the real world under the Golden Gate Bridge:
   a. WELL 1000
   b. ARPANET
   c. ITRW
   d. CMC

2. Reagan's experience in being a national spokesman for this company helped him become a significant public figure and perfect his style and conservative message:
   a. General Motors
   b. Westinghouse
   c. General Electric
   d. Chrysler

3. Which one of the following was NOT an "anti" element of Reagan's speeches?
   a. taxes
   b. government
   c. communism
   d. religion

4. If you were a believer in supply-side economics, then you would admire and want more of these:
   a. Steve Jobs/Nolan Bushnell
   b. Lee Atwater/Willie Horton
   c. Carter, Clinton/Panetta
   d. Oliver North/John Poindexter

5. The Omnibus Reconciliation Act of 1981
   a. cut over 200 social and cultural programs.
   b. also called Gramm-Rudman aimed at controlling the deficit.
   c. cut income and corporate taxes.
   d. deregulated numerous government agency rulings.

6. Which one of the following was NOT something that had already been increased by President Carter and continued by President Reagan?
   a. defense spending
   b. human resource spending
   c. revival of Cold War
   d. deregulation

7. Congress tried to control the problem of covert war in Nicaragua by passing the amendment known as
   a. Gramm-Rudman.
   b. Tower.
   c. Boland.
   d. Iran-Contra.

8. President Reagan's CBI meant
   a. Communist Barrier International.
   b. Cut Back Immigration.
   c. Compunications Belt Initiative.
   d. Caribbean Basin Initiative.

9. Which one of the following was NOT a Latin American area to which President Reagan sent military aid, advisors or troops?
   a. El Salvador
   b. Nicaragua
   c. Grenada
   d. Cuba

10. If you liked to live vicariously through what Tom Wolfe called plutography, then you liked watching
    a. commercials.
    b. Disney cartoons.
    c. lifestyles of the rich and famous.
    d. spectacular special effects and science fiction with traditional values.

11. ACT-UP, WHAM and the Quilt Project were all educational, political and fundraising efforts publicizing the problem of
    a. widespread drug use.
    b. AIDS.
    c. homelessness.
    d. continuing racial discrimination.

12. Lee Atwater claimed that if he could make this person a household name, he would win the election for Bush:
    a. Ivan Boesky
    b. Willie Horton
    c. Robert Bork
    d. Ollie North

13. The Persian Gulf War developed when Iraq invaded
    a. Iran.
    b. Kuwait.
    c. Saudi Arabia.
    d. Israel.

14. During the Persian Gulf War, these individuals were accompanied by "military escorts:"
    a. United Nations Officials
    b. Bedouins
    c. oil well personnel
    d. reporters

CHRONOLOGY AND MAPS:

15. MTV and CNN began broadcasting as cable channels in
    a. 1980.
    b. 1981.
    c. 1987.
    d. 1988.

16. Marines landed on Grenada and ousted the anti-American Marxist regime in
    a. 1983.
    b. 1984.
    c. 1986.
    d. 1987.

17. In the 1980 election, Republican candidate Reagan carried
    a. the Far West.
    b. the South.
    c. New England.
    d. all states but six.

18. Immigration to the United States from 1981 to 1989 came most heavily from
    a. Europe.   c. Asia.
    b. Latin America.   d. Africa.

SHORT ESSAY:

19. How did Gorbachev attempt to improve the Soviet Union's economic performance?

20. What were the major issues involved in the Iran-Contra Scandal?

21. Describe the major events in the collapse of communism during the late 1980s.

EXTENDED ESSAY:

22. In what ways did Reagan represent a departure from his immediate presidential predecessors? Why was this popular or beneficial to the country?

23. Why did the Reagan Administration believe U.S. interests were so greatly involved in Central America?

24. Analyze President Bush's drop in popularity from the end of the Gulf War until the 1992 election.

ANSWERS – CHAPTER 31

MULTIPLE CHOICE:
1. a, pp. 946-7	6. b, p. 955	11. b, p. 966
2. c, p. 949	7. c, p. 955	12. b, p. 970
3. d, p. 949	8. d, p. 955	13. b, p. 973
4. a, pp. 949-50	9. d, pp. 954-5	14. d, p. 974
5. a, p. 950	10. c, p. 964	

CHRONOLOGY AND MAPS:
15. b, p. 983	17. d, p. 949
16. a, p. 983	18. c, p. 970

SHORT ESSAY:
19-21

EXTENDED ESSAY:
22-24

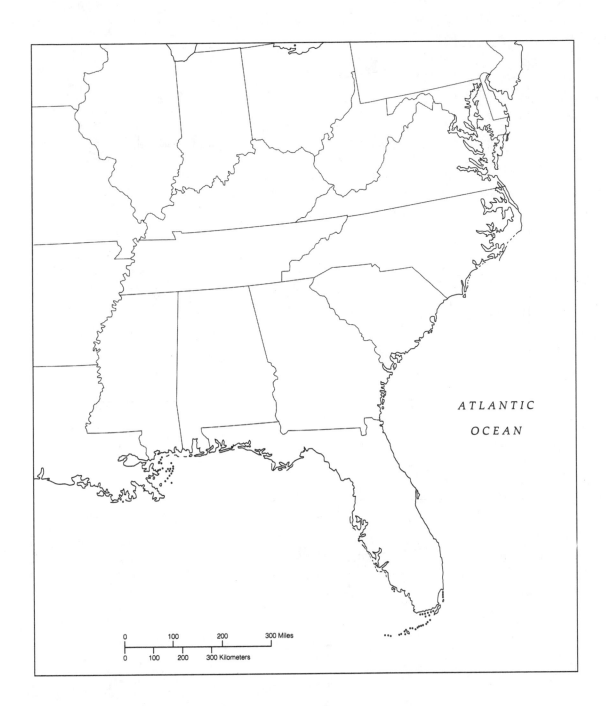

ATLANTIC

OCEAN

0   100   200   300 Miles

0   100   200   300 Kilometers

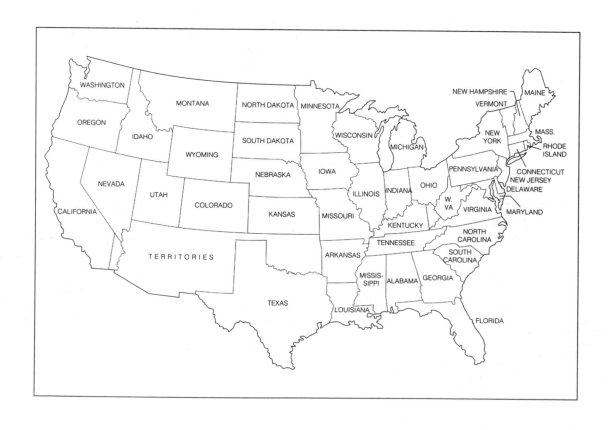

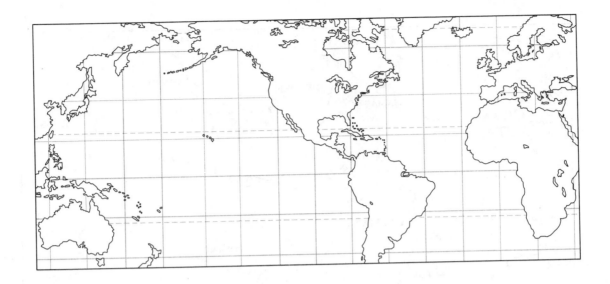

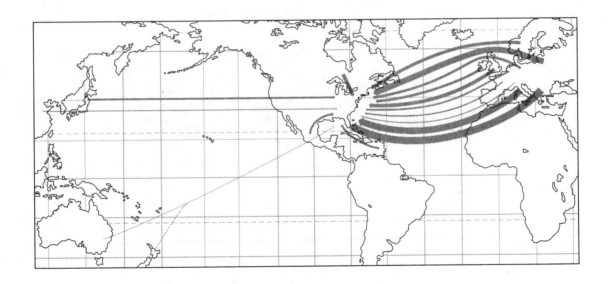

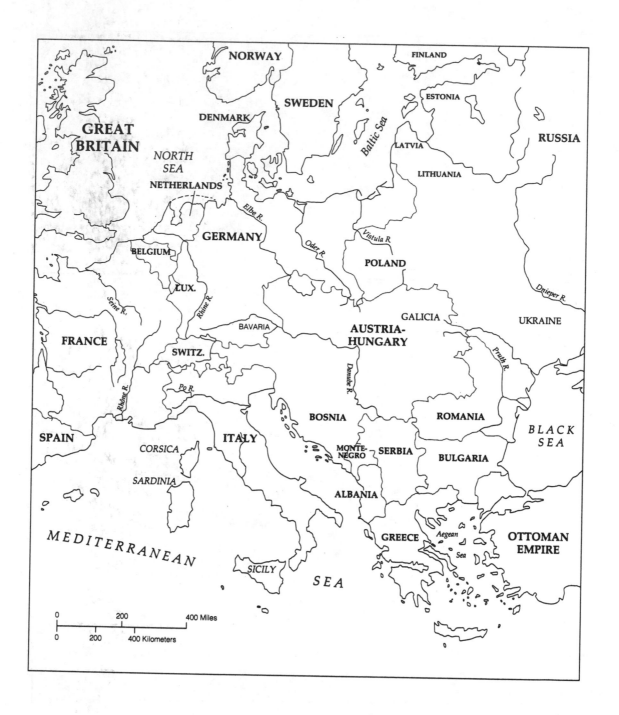

ATLANTIC OCEAN

GULF
OF
MEXICO

PACIFIC
OCEAN

CARIBBEAN
SEA

Lago
de Nigaragua

Lake
Maracaibo

0   200   400   600 Miles

0   600 Kilometers

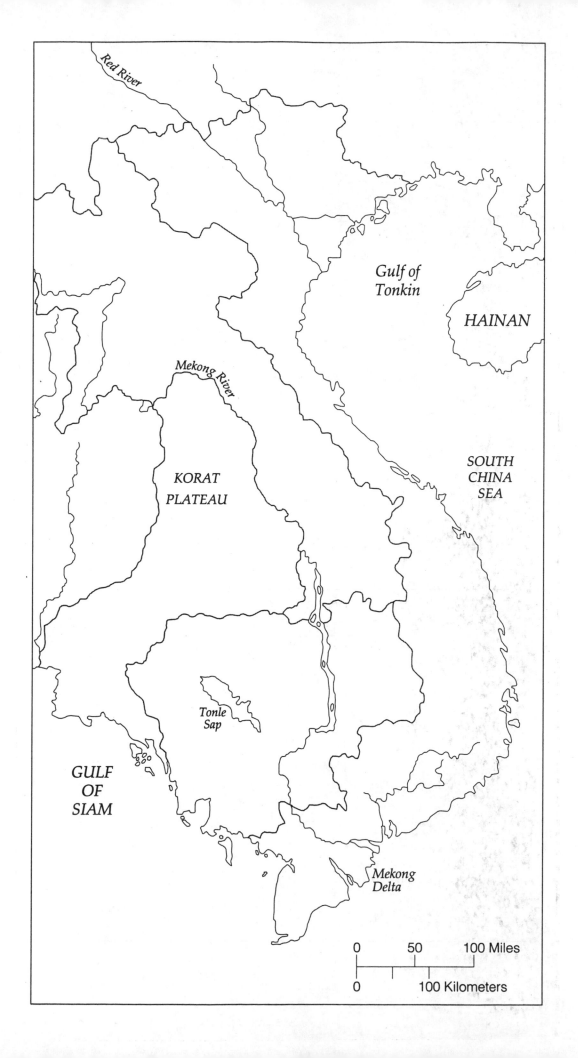

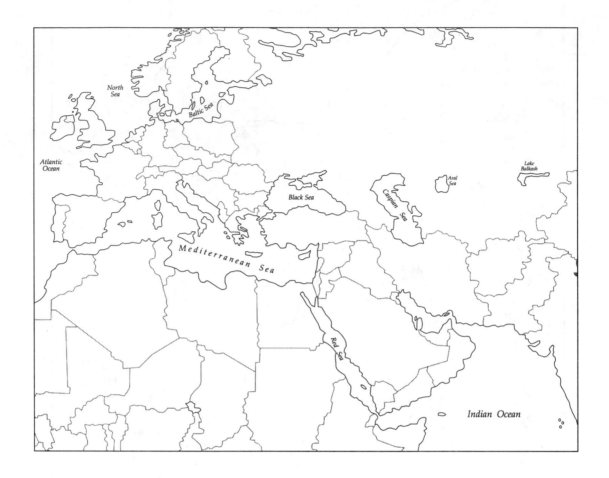

North
Sea

Baltic Sea

Atlantic
Ocean

Black Sea

Caspian Sea

Aral
Sea

Lake
Balkash

Mediterranean Sea

Red Sea

Indian Ocean